Table of Contents

Selected Chapters from

Operating System Concepts

Eighth Edition

ABRAHAM SILBERSCHATZ
Yale University

PETER BAER GALVIN
Corporate Technologies, Inc.

GREG GAGNE
Westminster College

WILEY *Custom*
LEARNING SOLUTIONS

This book was set in Palatino by the author using LaTeX and printed and bound by Victor Graphics. The cover was printed by Victor Graphics.

This book is printed on acid free paper.   ∞

ISBN: 978-0-470-92720-5

Printed in the United States of America

10 9 8 7 6 5 4 3

Operating System Concepts

Eighth Edition

ABRAHAM SILBERSCHATZ
Yale University

PETER BAER GALVIN
Corporate Technologies, Inc.

GREG GAGNE
Westminster College

JOHN WILEY & SONS. INC

ASSOCIATE PUBLISHER	Dan Sayre
EDITORIAL ASSISTANT	Carolyn Weisman
SENIOR PRODUCTION EDITOR	Ken Santor
COVER DESIGNER	Howard Grossman
COVER ILLUSTRATIONS	Susan Cyr
TEXT DESIGNER	Judy Allan

This book was set in Palatino by the author using LaTeX and printed and bound by R.R. Donnelley/Jefferson City. The cover was printed by R. R. Donnelley/Jefferson City

This book is printed on acid free paper. ∞

ISBN: 978-0-470-92720-5

Printed in the United States of America

10 9 8 7 6 5 4 3 2 1

To my children, Lemor, Sivan, and Aaron
and my Nicolette

Avi Silberschatz

To my wife, Carla,
and my children, Gwen, Owen, and Maddie

Peter Baer Galvin

To my wife, Pat,
and our sons, Tom and Jay

Greg Gagne

Abraham Silberschatz is the Sidney J. Weinberg Professor & Chair of Computer Science at Yale University. Prior to joining Yale, he was the Vice President of the Information Sciences Research Center at Bell Laboratories. Prior to that, he held a chaired professorship in the Department of Computer Sciences at the University of Texas at Austin.

Professor Silberschatz is an ACM Fellow and an IEEE Fellow. He received the 2002 IEEE Taylor L. Booth Education Award, the 1998 ACM Karl V. Karlstrom Outstanding Educator Award, and the 1997 ACM SIGMOD Contribution Award. In recognition of his outstanding level of innovation and technical excellence, he was awarded the Bell Laboratories President's Award for three different projects—the QTM Project (1998), the DataBlitz Project (1999), and the NetInventory Project (2004).

Professor Silberschatz' writings have appeared in numerous ACM and IEEE publications and other professional conferences and journals. He is a coauthor of the textbook *Database System Concepts*. He has also written Op-Ed articles for the New York Times, the Boston Globe, and the Hartford Courant, among others.

Peter Baer Galvin is the chief technologist for Corporate Technologies (www.cptech.com), a computer facility reseller and integrator. Before that, Mr. Galvin was the systems manager for Brown University's Computer Science Department. He is also Sun columnist for *;login:* magazine. Mr. Galvin has written articles for *Byte* and other magazines, and has written columns for *SunWorld* and *SysAdmin* magazines. As a consultant and trainer, he has given talks and taught tutorials on security and system administration worldwide.

Greg Gagne is chair of the Computer Science department at Westminster College in Salt Lake City where he has been teaching since 1990. In addition to teaching operating systems, he also teaches computer networks, distributed systems, and software engineering. He also provides workshops to computer science educators and industry professionals.

Preface

Operating systems are an essential part of any computer system. Similarly, a course on operating systems is an essential part of any computer-science education. This field is undergoing rapid change, as computers are now prevalent in virtually every application, from games for children through the most sophisticated planning tools for governments and multinational firms. Yet the fundamental concepts remain fairly clear, and it is on these that we base this book.

We wrote this book as a text for an introductory course in operating systems at the junior or senior undergraduate level or at the first-year graduate level. We hope that practitioners will also find it useful. It provides a clear description of the *concepts* that underlie operating systems. As prerequisites, we assume that the reader is familiar with basic data structures, computer organization, and a high-level language, such as C or Java. The hardware topics required for an understanding of operating systems are included in Chapter 1. For code examples, we use predominantly C, with some Java, but the reader can still understand the algorithms without a thorough knowledge of these languages.

Concepts are presented using intuitive descriptions. Important theoretical results are covered, but formal proofs are omitted. The bibliographical notes at the end of each chapter contain pointers to research papers in which results were first presented and proved, as well as references to material for further reading. In place of proofs, figures and examples are used to suggest why we should expect the result in question to be true.

The fundamental concepts and algorithms covered in the book are often based on those used in existing commercial operating systems. Our aim is to present these concepts and algorithms in a general setting that is not tied to one particular operating system. We present a large number of examples that pertain to the most popular and the most innovative operating systems, including Sun Microsystems' Solaris; Linux; Microsoft Windows Vista, Windows 2000, and Windows XP; and Apple Mac OS X. When we refer to Windows XP as an example operating system, we are implying Windows Vista, Windows XP, and Windows 2000. If a feature exists in a specific release, we state this explicitly.

Organization of This Book

The organization of this text reflects our many years of teaching courses on operating systems. Consideration was also given to the feedback provided by the reviewers of the text, as well as comments submitted by readers of earlier editions. In addition, the content of the text corresponds to the suggestions from *Computing Curricula 2005* for teaching operating systems, published by the Joint Task Force of the IEEE Computing Society and the Association for Computing Machinery (ACM).

On the supporting Web site for this text, we provide several sample syllabi that suggest various approaches for using the text in both introductory and advanced courses. As a general rule, we encourage readers to progress sequentially through the chapters, as this strategy provides the most thorough study of operating systems. However, by using the sample syllabi, a reader can select a different ordering of chapters (or subsections of chapters).

On-line support for the text is provided by WileyPLUS. On this site, students can find sample exercises and programming problems, and instructors can assign and grade problems. In addition, in WileyPLUS, students can access new operating-system simulators, which are used to work through exercises and hands-on lab activities. References to the simulators and associated activities appear at the ends of several chapters in the text.

Content of This Book

The text is organized in eight major parts:

- **Overview**. Chapters 1 and 2 explain what operating systems *are*, what they *do*, and how they are *designed* and *constructed*. These chapters discuss what the common features of an operating system are, what an operating system does for the user, and what it does for the computer-system operator. The presentation is motivational and explanatory in nature. We have avoided a discussion of how things are done internally in these chapters. Therefore, they are suitable for individual readers or for students in lower-level classes who want to learn what an operating system is without getting into the details of the internal algorithms.

- **Process management**. Chapters 3 through 7 describe the process concept and concurrency as the heart of modern operating systems. A *process* is the unit of work in a system. Such a system consists of a collection of *concurrently* executing processes, some of which are operating-system processes (those that execute system code) and the rest of which are user processes (those that execute user code). These chapters cover methods for process scheduling, interprocess communication, process synchronization, and deadlock handling. Also included is a discussion of threads, as well as an examination of issues related to multicore systems.

- **Memory management**. Chapters 8 and 9 deal with the management of main memory during the execution of a process. To improve both the utilization of the CPU and the speed of its response to its users, the computer must keep several processes in memory. There are many different memory-management schemes, reflecting various approaches to memory management, and the effectiveness of a particular algorithm depends on the situation.

- **Storage management.** Chapters 10 through 13 describe how the file system, mass storage, and I/O are handled in a modern computer system. The file system provides the mechanism for on-line storage of and access to both data and programs. We describe the classic internal algorithms and structures of storage management and provide a firm practical understanding of the algorithms used—their properties, advantages, and disadvantages. Our discussion of storage also includes matters related to secondary and tertiary storage. Since the I/O devices that attach to a computer vary widely, the operating system needs to provide a wide range of functionality to applications to allow them to control all aspects of these devices. We discuss system I/O in depth, including I/O system design, interfaces, and internal system structures and functions. In many ways, I/O devices are the slowest major components of the computer. Because they represent a performance bottleneck, we also examine performance issues associated with I/O devices.

- **Protection and security.** Chapters 14 and 15 discuss the mechanisms necessary for the protection and security of computer systems. The processes in an operating system must be protected from one another's activities, and to provide such protection, we must ensure that only processes that have gained proper authorization from the operating system can operate on the files, memory, CPU, and other resources of the system. Protection is a mechanism for controlling the access of programs, processes, or users to the resources defined by a computer system. This mechanism must provide a means of specifying the controls to be imposed, as well as a means of enforcement. Security protects the integrity of the information stored in the system (both data and code), as well as the physical resources of the system, from unauthorized access, malicious destruction or alteration, and accidental introduction of inconsistency.

- **Distributed systems.** Chapters 16 through 18 deal with a collection of processors that do not share memory or a clock—a *distributed system*. By providing the user with access to the various resources that it maintains, a distributed system can improve computation speed and data availability and reliability. Such a system also provides the user with a distributed file system, which is a file-service system whose users, servers, and storage devices are dispersed among the sites of a distributed system. A distributed system must provide various mechanisms for process synchronization and communication, as well as for dealing with deadlock problems and a variety of failures that are not encountered in a centralized system.

- **Special-purpose systems.** Chapters 19 and 20 deal with systems used for specific purposes, including real-time systems and multimedia systems. These systems have specific requirements that differ from those of the general-purpose systems that are the focus of the remainder of the text. Real-time systems may require not only that computed results be "correct" but also that the results be produced within a specified deadline period. Multimedia systems require quality-of-service guarantees ensuring that the multimedia data are delivered to clients within a specific time frame.

- **Case studies**. Chapters 21 through 23 in the book, and Appendices A through C (which are available on www.wiley.com/college/silberschatz and in WileyPLUS), integrate the concepts described in the earlier chapters by describing real operating systems. These systems include Linux, Windows XP, FreeBSD, Mach, and Windows 2000. We chose Linux and FreeBSD because UNIX—at one time—was almost small enough to understand yet was not a "toy" operating system. Most of its internal algorithms were selected for *simplicity*, rather than for speed or sophistication. Both Linux and FreeBSD are readily available to computer-science departments, so many students have access to these systems. We chose Windows XP and Windows 2000 because they provide an opportunity for us to study a modern operating system with a design and implementation drastically different from those of UNIX. Chapter 23 briefly describes a few other influential operating systems.

Operating-System Environments

This book uses examples of many real-world operating systems to illustrate fundamental operating-system concepts. However, particular attention is paid to the Microsoft family of operating systems (including Windows Vista, Windows 2000, and Windows XP) and various versions of UNIX (including Solaris, BSD, and Mac OS X). We also provide a significant amount of coverage of the Linux operating system reflecting the most recent version of the kernel —Version 2.6—at the time this book was written.

The text also provides several example programs written in C and Java. These programs are intended to run in the following programming environments:

- **Windows systems**. The primary programming environment for Windows systems is the Win32 API (application programming interface), which provides a comprehensive set of functions for managing processes, threads, memory, and peripheral devices. We provide several C programs illustrating the use of the Win32 API. Example programs were tested on systems running Windows Vista, Windows 2000, and Windows XP.

- **POSIX**. POSIX (which stands for *Portable Operating System Interface*) represents a set of standards implemented primarily for UNIX-based operating systems. Although Windows Vista, Windows XP, and Windows 2000 systems can also run certain POSIX programs, our coverage of POSIX focuses primarily on UNIX and Linux systems. POSIX-compliant systems must implement the POSIX core standard (POSIX.1): Linux, Solaris, and Mac OS X are examples of POSIX-compliant systems. POSIX also defines several extensions to the standards, including real-time extensions (POSIX1.b) and an extension for a threads library (POSIX1.c, better known as Pthreads). We provide several programming examples written in C illustrating the POSIX base API, as well as Pthreads and the extensions for real-time programming. These example programs were tested on Debian Linux 2.4 and 2.6 systems, Mac OS X 10.5, and Solaris 10 using the gcc 3.3 and 4.0 compilers.

- **Java**. Java is a widely used programming language with a rich API and built-in language support for thread creation and management. Java programs run on any operating system supporting a Java virtual machine (or JVM). We illustrate various operating system and networking concepts with several Java programs tested using the Java 1.5 JVM.

We have chosen these three programming environments because it is our opinion that they best represent the two most popular models of operating systems: Windows and UNIX/Linux, along with the widely used Java environment. Most programming examples are written in C, and we expect readers to be comfortable with this language; readers familiar with both the C and Java languages should easily understand most programs provided in this text.

In some instances—such as thread creation—we illustrate a specific concept using all three programming environments, allowing the reader to contrast the three different libraries as they address the same task. In other situations, we may use just one of the APIs to demonstrate a concept. For example, we illustrate shared memory using just the POSIX API; socket programming in TCP/IP is highlighted using the Java API.

The Eighth Edition

As we wrote the Eighth Edition of *Operating System Concepts*, we were guided by the many comments and suggestions we received from readers of our previous editions, as well as by our own observations about the rapidly changing fields of operating systems and networking. We have rewritten material in most of the chapters by bringing older material up to date and removing material that was no longer of interest or relevance.

We have made substantive revisions and organizational changes in many of the chapters. Most importantly, we have added coverage of open-source operating systems in Chapter 1. We have also added more practice exercises for students and included solutions in WileyPLUS, which also includes new simulators to provide demonstrations of operating-system operation. Below, we provide a brief outline of the major changes to the various chapters:

- **Chapter 1, Introduction,** has been expanded to include multicore CPUs, clustered computers, and open-source operating systems.

- **Chapter 2, Operating-System Structures,** provides significantly updated coverage of virtual machines, as well as multicore CPUs, the GRUB boot loader, and operating-system debugging.

- **Chapter 3, Processes,** provides new coverage of pipes as a form of interprocess communication.

- **Chapter 4, Threads,** adds new coverage of programming for multicore systems.

- **Chapter 5, CPU Scheduling,** adds coverage of virtual machine scheduling and multithreaded, multicore architectures.

- **Chapter 6, Process Synchronization,** adds a discussion of mutual exclusion locks, priority inversion, and transactional memory.

- **Chapter 8, Main Memory,** includes discussion of NUMA.

- **Chapter 9, Virtual Memory,** updates the Solaris example to include Solaris 10 memory management.

- **Chapter 10, File-System Interface,** is updated with current technologies and capacities.

- **Chapter 11, File-System Implementation,** includes a full description of Sun's ZFS file system and expands the coverage of volumes and directories.

- **Chapter 12, Mass-Storage Structure,** adds coverage of iSCSI, volumes, and ZFS pools.

- **Chapter 13, I/O Systems,** adds coverage of PCIX PCI Express, and Hyper-Transport.

- **Chapter 16, Distributed System Structures,** adds coverage of 802.11 wireless networks.

- **Chapter 21, The Linux System,** has been updated to cover the latest version of the Linux kernel.

- **Chapter 23, Influential Operating Systems,** increases coverage of very early computers as well as TOPS-20, CP/M, MS-DOS, Windows, and the original Mac OS.

Programming Problems and Projects

To emphasize the concepts presented in the text, we have added several programming problems and projects that use the POSIX and Win32 APIs, as well as Java. We have added more than 15 new programming problems, which emphasize processes, threads, shared memory, process synchronization, and networking. In addition, we have added or modified several programming projects that are more involved than standard programming exercises. These projects include adding a system call to the Linux kernel, using pipes on both UNIX and Windows systems, using UNIX message queues, creating multithreaded applications, and solving the producer–consumer problem using shared memory.

The Eighth Edition also incorporates a set of operating-system simulators designed by Steven Robbins of the University of Texas at San Antonio. The simulators are intended to model the behavior of an operating system as it performs various tasks, such as CPU and disk-head scheduling, process creation and interprocess communication, starvation, and address translation. These simulators are written in Java and will run on any computer system with Java 1.4. Students can download the simulators from WileyPLUS and observe the behavior of several operating system concepts in various scenarios. In addition, each simulator includes several exercises that ask students to set certain parameters of the simulator, observe how the system behaves, and then explain this behavior. These exercises can be assigned through WileyPLUS. The WileyPLUS course also includes algorithmic problems and tutorials developed by Scott M. Pike of Texas A&M University.

Teaching Supplements

The following teaching supplements are available in WileyPLUS and on www.wiley.com/college/silberschatz: a set of slides to accompany the book, model course syllabi, all C and Java source code, up-to-date errata, three case study appendices and the Distributed Communication appendix. The WileyPLUS course also contains the simulators and associated exercises, additional practice exercises (with solutions) not found in the text, and a testbank of additional problems. Students are encouraged to solve the practice exercises on their own and then use the provided solutions to check their own answers.

To obtain restricted supplements, such as the solution guide to the exercises in the text, contact your local John Wiley & Sons sales representative. Note that these supplements are available only to faculty who use this text. You can find your Wiley representative by going to www.wiley.com/college and clicking "Who's my rep?"

Mailing List

We use the mailman system for communication among the users of *Operating System Concepts*. If you wish to use this facility, please visit the following URL and follow the instructions there to subscribe:

http://mailman.cs.yale.edu/mailman/listinfo/os-book

The mailman mailing-list system provides many benefits, such as an archive of postings, as well as several subscription options, including digest and Web only. To send messages to the list, send e-mail to:

os-book@cs.yale.edu

Depending on the message, we will either reply to you personally or forward the message to everyone on the mailing list. The list is moderated, so you will receive no inappropriate mail.

Students who are using this book as a text for class should not use the list to ask for answers to the exercises. They will not be provided.

Suggestions

We have attempted to clean up every error in this new edition, but—as happens with operating systems—a few obscure bugs may remain. We would appreciate hearing from you about any textual errors or omissions that you identify.

If you would like to suggest improvements or to contribute exercises, we would also be glad to hear from you. Please send correspondence to os-book-authors@cs.yale.edu.

Acknowledgments

This book is derived from the previous editions, the first three of which were coauthored by James Peterson. Others who helped us with previous editions include Hamid Arabnia, Rida Bazzi, Randy Bentson, David Black, Joseph Boykin, Jeff Brumfield, Gael Buckley, Roy Campbell, P. C. Capon, John Carpenter, Gil Carrick, Thomas Casavant, Bart Childs, Ajoy Kumar Datta, Joe Deck, Sudarshan K. Dhall, Thomas Doeppner, Caleb Drake, M. Racsit Eskicioğlu, Hans Flack, Robert Fowler, G. Scott Graham, Richard Guy, Max Hailperin, Rebecca Hartman, Wayne Hathaway, Christopher Haynes, Don Heller, Bruce Hillyer, Mark Holliday, Dean Hougen, Michael Huangs, Ahmed Kamel, Morty Kewstel, Richard Kieburtz, Carol Kroll, Morty Kwestel, Thomas LeBlanc, John Leggett, Jerrold Leichter, Ted Leung, Gary Lippman, Carolyn Miller, Michael Molloy, Euripides Montagne, Yoichi Muraoka, Jim M. Ng, Banu Özden, Ed Posnak, Boris Putanec, Charles Qualline, John Quarterman, Mike Reiter, Gustavo Rodriguez-Rivera, Carolyn J. C. Schauble, Thomas P. Skinner, Yannis Smaragdakis, Jesse St. Laurent, John Stankovic, Adam Stauffer, Steven Stepanek, John Sterling, Hal Stern, Louis Stevens, Pete Thomas, David Umbaugh, Steve Vinoski, Tommy Wagner, Larry L. Wear, John Werth, James M. Westall, J. S. Weston, and Yang Xiang

Parts of Chapter 12 were derived from a paper by Hillyer and Silberschatz [1996]. Parts of Chapter 17 were derived from a paper by Levy and Silberschatz [1990]. Chapter 21 was derived from an unpublished manuscript by Stephen Tweedie. Chapter 22 was derived from an unpublished manuscript by Dave Probert, Cliff Martin, and Avi Silberschatz. Appendix C was derived from an unpublished manuscript by Cliff Martin. Cliff Martin also helped with updating the UNIX appendix to cover FreeBSD. Some of the exercises and accompanying solutions were supplied by Arvind Krishnamurthy.

Mike Shapiro, Bryan Cantrill, and Jim Mauro answered several Solaris-related questions. Bryan Cantrill from Sun Microsystems helped with the ZFS coverage. Steve Robbins of the University of Texas at San Antonio designed the set of simulators that we incorporate in WileyPLUS. Reece Newman of Westminster College initially explored this set of simulators and their appropriateness for this text. Josh Dees and Rob Reynolds contributed coverage of Microsoft's .NET. The project for POSIX message queues was contributed by John Trono of Saint Michael's College in Colchester, Vermont.

Marilyn Turnamian helped generate figures and presentation slides. Mark Wogahn has made sure that the software to produce the book (e.g., Latex macros, fonts) works properly.

Our Associate Publisher, Dan Sayre, provided expert guidance as we prepared this edition. He was assisted by Carolyn Weisman, who managed many details of this project smoothly. The Senior Production Editor Ken Santor, was instrumental in handling all the production details. Lauren Sapira and Cindy Johnson have been very helpful with getting material ready and available for WileyPlus.

The cover illustrator was Susan Cyr, and the cover designer was Howard Grossman. Beverly Peavler copy-edited the manuscript. The freelance proof-reader was Katrina Avery; the freelance indexer was WordCo, Inc.

Abraham Silberschatz, New Haven, CT, 2008
Peter Baer Galvin, Burlington, MA, 2008
Greg Gagne, Salt Lake City, UT, 2008

Part One

Overview

An *operating system* acts as an intermediary between the user of a computer and the computer hardware. The purpose of an operating system is to provide an environment in which a user can execute programs in a *convenient* and *efficient* manner.

An operating system is software that manages the computer hardware. The hardware must provide appropriate mechanisms to ensure the correct operation of the computer system and to prevent user programs from interfering with the proper operation of the system.

Internally, operating systems vary greatly in their makeup, since they are organized along many different lines. The design of a new operating system is a major task. It is important that the goals of the system be well defined before the design begins. These goals form the basis for choices among various algorithms and strategies.

Because an operating system is large and complex, it must be created piece by piece. Each of these pieces should be a well delineated portion of the system, with carefully defined inputs, outputs, and functions.

CHAPTER

Introduction

An **operating system** is a program that manages the computer hardware. It also provides a basis for application programs and acts as an intermediary between the computer user and the computer hardware. An amazing aspect of operating systems is how varied they are in accomplishing these tasks. Mainframe operating systems are designed primarily to optimize utilization of hardware. Personal computer (PC) operating systems support complex games, business applications, and everything in between. Operating systems for handheld computers are designed to provide an environment in which a user can easily interface with the computer to execute programs. Thus, some operating systems are designed to be *convenient*, others to be *efficient*, and others some combination of the two.

Before we can explore the details of computer system operation, we need to know something about system structure. We begin by discussing the basic functions of system startup, I/O, and storage. We also describe the basic computer architecture that makes it possible to write a functional operating system.

Because an operating system is large and complex, it must be created piece by piece. Each of these pieces should be a well-delineated portion of the system, with carefully defined inputs, outputs, and functions. In this chapter, we provide a general overview of the major components of an operating system.

CHAPTER OBJECTIVES

- To provide a grand tour of the major components of operating systems.
- To describe the basic organization of computer systems.

1.1 What Operating Systems Do

We begin our discussion by looking at the operating system's role in the overall computer system. A computer system can be divided roughly into

3

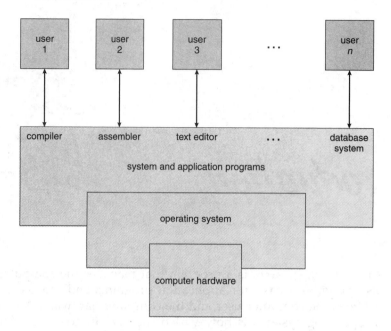

Figure 1.1 Abstract view of the components of a computer system.

four components: the *hardware,* the *operating system,* the *application programs,* and the *users* (Figure 1.1).

The **hardware**—the **central processing unit (CPU)**, the **memory**, and the **input/output (I/O) devices**—provides the basic computing resources for the system. The **application programs**—such as word processors, spreadsheets, compilers, and Web browsers—define the ways in which these resources are used to solve users' computing problems. The operating system controls the hardware and coordinates its use among the various application programs for the various users.

We can also view a computer system as consisting of hardware, software, and data. The operating system provides the means for proper use of these resources in the operation of the computer system. An operating system is similar to a *government*. Like a government, it performs no useful function by itself. It simply provides an *environment* within which other programs can do useful work.

To understand more fully the operating system's role, we next explore operating systems from two viewpoints: that of the user and that of the system.

1.1.1 User View

The user's view of the computer varies according to the interface being used. Most computer users sit in front of a PC, consisting of a monitor, keyboard, mouse, and system unit. Such a system is designed for one user to monopolize its resources. The goal is to maximize the work (or play) that the user is performing. In this case, the operating system is designed mostly for **ease of use**, with some attention paid to performance and none paid to **resource utilization**—how various hardware and software resources are shared. Performance is, of course, important to the user; but such systems are optimized for the single-user experience rather than the requirements of multiple users.

In other cases, a user sits at a terminal connected to a **mainframe** or a **minicomputer**. Other users are accessing the same computer through other terminals. These users share resources and may exchange information. The operating system in such cases is designed to maximize resource utilization— to assure that all available CPU time, memory, and I/O are used efficiently and that no individual user takes more than her fair share.

In still other cases, users sit at **workstations** connected to networks of other workstations and **servers**. These users have dedicated resources at their disposal, but they also share resources such as networking and servers—file, compute, and print servers. Therefore, their operating system is designed to compromise between individual usability and resource utilization.

Recently, many varieties of handheld computers have come into fashion. Most of these devices are standalone units for individual users. Some are connected to networks, either directly by wire or (more often) through wireless modems and networking. Because of power, speed, and interface limitations, they perform relatively few remote operations. Their operating systems are designed mostly for individual usability, but performance per unit of battery life is important as well.

Some computers have little or no user view. For example, embedded computers in home devices and automobiles may have numeric keypads and may turn indicator lights on or off to show status, but they and their operating systems are designed primarily to run without user intervention.

1.1.2 System View

From the computer's point of view, the operating system is the program most intimately involved with the hardware. In this context, we can view an operating system as a **resource allocator**. A computer system has many resources that may be required to solve a problem: CPU time, memory space, file-storage space, I/O devices, and so on. The operating system acts as the manager of these resources. Facing numerous and possibly conflicting requests for resources, the operating system must decide how to allocate them to specific programs and users so that it can operate the computer system efficiently and fairly. As we have seen, resource allocation is especially important where many users access the same mainframe or minicomputer.

A slightly different view of an operating system emphasizes the need to control the various I/O devices and user programs. An operating system is a control program. A **control program** manages the execution of user programs to prevent errors and improper use of the computer. It is especially concerned with the operation and control of I/O devices.

1.1.3 Defining Operating Systems

We have looked at the operating system's role from the views of the user and of the system. How, though, can we define what an operating system is? In general, we have no completely adequate definition of an operating system. Operating systems exist because they offer a reasonable way to solve the problem of creating a usable computing system. The fundamental goal of computer systems is to execute user programs and to make solving user

---

STORAGE DEFINITIONS AND NOTATION

A bit is the basic unit of computer storage. It can contain one of two values, zero and one. All other storage in a computer is based on collections of bits. Given enough bits, it is amazing how many things a computer can represent: numbers, letters, images, movies, sounds, documents, and programs, to name a few. A byte is 8 bits, and on most computers it is the smallest convenient chunk of storage. For example, most computers don't have an instruction to move a bit but do have one to move a byte. A less common term is word, which is a given computer architecture's native storage unit. A word is generally made up of one or more bytes. For example, a computer may have instructions to move 64-bit (8-byte) words.

A kilobyte, or KB, is 1,024 bytes; a megabyte, or MB, is $1,024^2$ bytes; and a gigabyte, or GB, is $1,024^3$ bytes. Computer manufacturers often round off these numbers and say that a megabyte is 1 million bytes and a gigabyte is 1 billion bytes.

---

problems easier. Toward this goal, computer hardware is constructed. Since bare hardware alone is not particularly easy to use, application programs are developed. These programs require certain common operations, such as those controlling the I/O devices. The common functions of controlling and allocating resources are then brought together into one piece of software: the operating system.

In addition, we have no universally accepted definition of what is part of the operating system. A simple viewpoint is that it includes everything a vendor ships when you order "the operating system." The features included, however, vary greatly across systems. Some systems take up less than 1 megabyte of space and lack even a full-screen editor, whereas others require gigabytes of space and are entirely based on graphical windowing systems. A more common definition, and the one that we usually follow, is that the operating system is the one program running at all times on the computer—usually called the kernel. (Along with the kernel, there are two other types of programs: systems programs, which are associated with the operating system but are not part of the kernel, and application programs, which include all programs not associated with the operation of the system.)

The matter of what constitutes an operating system has become increasingly important. In 1998, the United States Department of Justice filed suit against Microsoft, in essence claiming that Microsoft included too much functionality in its operating systems and thus prevented application vendors from competing. For example, a Web browser was an integral part of the operating systems. As a result, Microsoft was found guilty of using its operating-system monopoly to limit competition.

1.2   Computer-System Organization

Before we can explore the details of how computer systems operate, we need general knowledge of the structure of a computer system. In this section, we look at several parts of this structure. The section is mostly concerned

THE STUDY OF OPERATING SYSTEMS

There has never been a more interesting time to study operating systems, and it has never been easier. The open-source movement has overtaken operating systems, causing many of them to be made available in both source and binary (executable) format. This list includes Linux, BSD UNIX, Solaris, and part of Mac OS X. The availability of source code allows us to study operating systems from the inside out. Questions that previously could only be answered by looking at documentation or the behavior of an operating system can now be answered by examining the code itself.

In addition, the rise of virtualization as a mainstream (and frequently free) computer function makes it possible to run many operating systems on top of one core system. For example, VMware (http://www.vmware.com) provides a free "player" on which hundreds of free "virtual appliances" can run. Using this method, students can try out hundreds of operating systems within their existing operating systems at no cost.

Operating systems that are no longer commercially viable have been open-sourced as well, enabling us to study how systems operated in a time of fewer CPU, memory, and storage resources. An extensive but not complete list of open-source operating-system projects is available from http://dmoz.org/Computers/Software/Operating_Systems/Open_Source/. Simulators of specific hardware are also available in some cases, allowing the operating system to run on "native" hardware, all within the confines of a modern computer and modern operating system. For example, a DECSYSTEM-20 simulator running on Mac OS X can boot TOPS-20, load the source tapes, and modify and compile a new TOPS-20 kernel. An interested student can search the Internet to find the original papers that describe the operating system and the original manuals.

The advent of open-source operating systems also makes it easy to make the move from student to operating-system developer. With some knowledge, some effort, and an Internet connection, a student can even create a new operating-system distribution! Just a few years, ago it was difficult or impossible to get access to source code. Now that access is limited only by how much time and disk space a student has.

with computer-system organization, so you can skim or skip it if you already understand the concepts.

1.2.1 Computer-System Operation

A modern general-purpose computer system consists of one or more CPUs and a number of device controllers connected through a common bus that provides access to shared memory (Figure 1.2). Each device controller is in charge of a specific type of device (for example, disk drives, audio devices, and video displays). The CPU and the device controllers can execute concurrently, competing for memory cycles. To ensure orderly access to the shared memory, a memory controller is provided whose function is to synchronize access to the memory.

For a computer to start running—for instance, when it is powered up or rebooted—it needs to have an initial program to run. This initial

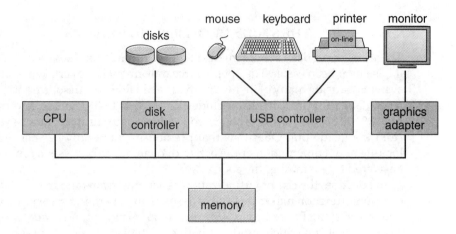

Figure 1.2 A modern computer system.

program, or **bootstrap program**, tends to be simple. Typically, it is stored in read-only memory (ROM) or electrically erasable programmable read-only memory (EEPROM), known by the general term **firmware**, within the computer hardware. It initializes all aspects of the system, from CPU registers to device controllers to memory contents. The bootstrap program must know how to load the operating system and how to start executing that system. To accomplish this goal, the bootstrap program must locate and load into memory the operating-system kernel. The operating system then starts executing the first process, such as "init," and waits for some event to occur.

The occurrence of an event is usually signaled by an **interrupt** from either the hardware or the software. Hardware may trigger an interrupt at any time by sending a signal to the CPU, usually by way of the system bus. Software may trigger an interrupt by executing a special operation called a **system call** (also called a **monitor call**).

When the CPU is interrupted, it stops what it is doing and immediately transfers execution to a fixed location. The fixed location usually contains the starting address where the service routine for the interrupt is located. The interrupt service routine executes; on completion, the CPU resumes the interrupted computation. A time line of this operation is shown in Figure 1.3.

Interrupts are an important part of a computer architecture. Each computer design has its own interrupt mechanism, but several functions are common. The interrupt must transfer control to the appropriate interrupt service routine. The straightforward method for handling this transfer would be to invoke a generic routine to examine the interrupt information; the routine, in turn, would call the interrupt-specific handler. However, interrupts must be handled quickly. Since only a predefined number of interrupts is possible, a table of pointers to interrupt routines can be used instead to provide the necessary speed. The interrupt routine is called indirectly through the table, with no intermediate routine needed. Generally, the table of pointers is stored in low memory (the first hundred or so locations). These locations hold the addresses of the interrupt service routines for the various devices. This array, or **interrupt vector**, of addresses is then indexed by a unique device number, given with the interrupt request, to provide the address of the interrupt service routine for

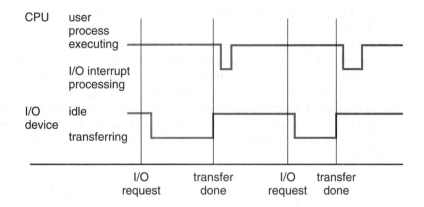

Figure 1.3 Interrupt time line for a single process doing output.

the interrupting device. Operating systems as different as Windows and UNIX dispatch interrupts in this manner.

The interrupt architecture must also save the address of the interrupted instruction. Many old designs simply stored the interrupt address in a fixed location or in a location indexed by the device number. More recent architectures store the return address on the system stack. If the interrupt routine needs to modify the processor state—for instance, by modifying register values—it must explicitly save the current state and then restore that state before returning. After the interrupt is serviced, the saved return address is loaded into the program counter, and the interrupted computation resumes as though the interrupt had not occurred.

1.2.2 Storage Structure

The CPU can load instructions only from memory, so any programs to run must be stored there. General-purpose computers run most of their programs from rewriteable memory, called main memory (also called **random-access memory** or **RAM**). Main memory commonly is implemented in a semiconductor technology called dynamic random-access memory (DRAM). Computers use other forms of memory as well. Because the read-only memory (ROM) cannot be changed, only static programs are stored there. The immutability of ROM is of use in game cartridges. EEPROM cannot be changed frequently and so contains mostly static programs. For example, smartphones have EEPROM to store their factory-installed programs.

All forms of memory provide an array of words. Each word has its own address. Interaction is achieved through a sequence of load or store instructions to specific memory addresses. The load instruction moves a word from main memory to an internal register within the CPU, whereas the store instruction moves the content of a register to main memory. Aside from explicit loads and stores, the CPU automatically loads instructions from main memory for execution.

A typical instruction–execution cycle, as executed on a system with a **von Neumann** architecture, first fetches an instruction from memory and stores that instruction in the **instruction register**. The instruction is then decoded and may cause operands to be fetched from memory and stored in some internal register. After the instruction on the operands has been executed, the result may be stored back in memory. Notice that the memory unit sees only a stream of memory addresses; it does not know how they are generated (by the instruction counter, indexing, indirection, literal addresses, or some other means) or what they are for (instructions or data). Accordingly, we can ignore *how* a memory address is generated by a program. We are interested only in the sequence of memory addresses generated by the running program.

Ideally, we want the programs and data to reside in main memory permanently. This arrangement usually is not possible for the following two reasons:

1. Main memory is usually too small to store all needed programs and data permanently.

2. Main memory is a *volatile* storage device that loses its contents when power is turned off or otherwise lost.

Thus, most computer systems provide secondary storage as an extension of main memory. The main requirement for secondary storage is that it be able to hold large quantities of data permanently.

The most common secondary-storage device is a magnetic disk, which provides storage for both programs and data. Most programs (system and application) are stored on a disk until they are loaded into memory. Many programs then use the disk as both the source and the destination of their processing. Hence, the proper management of disk storage is of central importance to a computer system, as we discuss in Chapter 12.

In a larger sense, however, the storage structure that we have described—consisting of registers, main memory, and magnetic disks—is only one of many possible storage systems. Others include cache memory, CD-ROM, magnetic tapes, and so on. Each storage system provides the basic functions of storing a datum and holding that datum until it is retrieved at a later time. The main differences among the various storage systems lie in speed, cost, size, and volatility.

The wide variety of storage systems in a computer system can be organized in a hierarchy (Figure 1.4) according to speed and cost. The higher levels are expensive, but they are fast. As we move down the hierarchy, the cost per bit generally decreases, whereas the access time generally increases. This trade-off is reasonable; if a given storage system were both faster and less expensive than another—other properties being the same—then there would be no reason to use the slower, more expensive memory. In fact, many early storage devices, including paper tape and core memories, are relegated to museums now that magnetic tape and semiconductor memory have become faster and cheaper. The top four levels of memory in Figure 1.4 may be constructed using semiconductor memory.

In addition to differing in speed and cost, the various storage systems are either volatile or nonvolatile. As mentioned earlier, volatile storage loses its contents when the power to the device is removed. In the absence of expensive battery and generator backup systems, data must be written to nonvolatile storage for safekeeping. In the hierarchy shown in Figure 1.4, the storage systems above the electronic disk are volatile, whereas those below

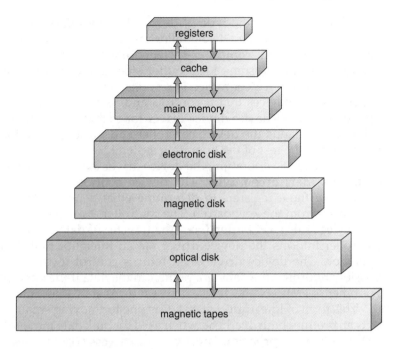

Figure 1.4 Storage-device hierarchy.

are nonvolatile. An electronic disk can be designed to be either volatile or nonvolatile. During normal operation, the electronic disk stores data in a large DRAM array, which is volatile. But many electronic-disk devices contain a hidden magnetic hard disk and a battery for backup power. If external power is interrupted, the electronic-disk controller copies the data from RAM to the magnetic disk. When external power is restored, the controller copies the data back into RAM. Another form of electronic disk is flash memory, which is popular in cameras and personal digital assistants (PDAs), in robots, and increasingly as removable storage on general-purpose computers. Flash memory is slower than DRAM but needs no power to retain its contents. Another form of nonvolatile storage is NVRAM, which is DRAM with battery backup power. This memory can be as fast as DRAM and (as long as the battery lasts) is nonvolatile.

The design of a complete memory system must balance all the factors just discussed: it must use only as much expensive memory as necessary while providing as much inexpensive, nonvolatile memory as possible. Caches can be installed to improve performance where a large access-time or transfer-rate disparity exists between two components.

1.2.3 I/O Structure

Storage is only one of many types of I/O devices within a computer. A large portion of operating system code is dedicated to managing I/O, both because of its importance to the reliability and performance of a system and because of the varying nature of the devices. Next, we provide an overview of I/O.

A general-purpose computer system consists of CPUs and multiple device controllers that are connected through a common bus. Each device controller is in charge of a specific type of device. Depending on the controller, more than one device may be attached. For instance, seven or more devices can be attached to the **small computer-systems interface (SCSI)** controller. A device controller maintains some local buffer storage and a set of special-purpose registers. The device controller is responsible for moving the data between the peripheral devices that it controls and its local buffer storage. Typically, operating systems have a **device driver** for each device controller. This device driver understands the device controller and presents a uniform interface to the device to the rest of the operating system.

To start an I/O operation, the device driver loads the appropriate registers within the device controller. The device controller, in turn, examines the contents of these registers to determine what action to take (such as "read a character from the keyboard"). The controller starts the transfer of data from the device to its local buffer. Once the transfer of data is complete, the device controller informs the device driver via an interrupt that it has finished its operation. The device driver then returns control to the operating system, possibly returning the data or a pointer to the data if the operation was a read. For other operations, the device driver returns status information.

This form of interrupt-driven I/O is fine for moving small amounts of data but can produce high overhead when used for bulk data movement such as disk I/O. To solve this problem, **direct memory access (DMA)** is used. After setting up buffers, pointers, and counters for the I/O device, the device controller transfers an entire block of data directly to or from its own buffer storage to memory, with no intervention by the CPU. Only one interrupt is generated per block, to tell the device driver that the operation has completed, rather than the one interrupt per byte generated for low-speed devices. While the device controller is performing these operations, the CPU is available to accomplish other work.

Some high-end systems use switch rather than bus architecture. On these systems, multiple components can talk to other components concurrently, rather than competing for cycles on a shared bus. In this case, DMA is even more effective. Figure 1.5 shows the interplay of all components of a computer system.

1.3 Computer-System Architecture

In Section 1.2, we introduced the general structure of a typical computer system. A computer system may be organized in a number of different ways, which we can categorize roughly according to the number of general-purpose processors used.

1.3.1 Single-Processor Systems

Most systems use a single processor. The variety of single-processor systems may be surprising, however, since these systems range from PDAs through mainframes. On a single-processor system, there is one main CPU capable of executing a general-purpose instruction set, including instructions from user processes. Almost all systems have other special-purpose processors as well. They may come in the form of device-specific processors, such as disk,

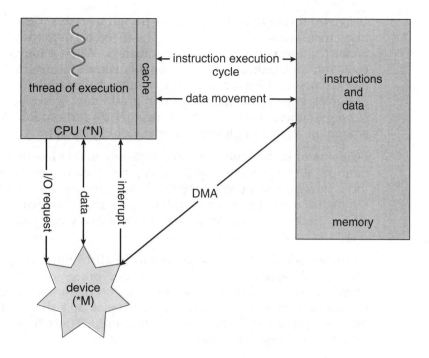

Figure 1.5 How a modern computer system works.

keyboard, and graphics controllers; or, on mainframes, they may come in the form of more general-purpose processors, such as I/O processors that move data rapidly among the components of the system.

All of these special-purpose processors run a limited instruction set and do not run user processes. Sometimes they are managed by the operating system, in that the operating system sends them information about their next task and monitors their status. For example, a disk-controller microprocessor receives a sequence of requests from the main CPU and implements its own disk queue and scheduling algorithm. This arrangement relieves the main CPU of the overhead of disk scheduling. PCs contain a microprocessor in the keyboard to convert the keystrokes into codes to be sent to the CPU. In other systems or circumstances, special-purpose processors are low-level components built into the hardware. The operating system cannot communicate with these processors; they do their jobs autonomously. The use of special-purpose microprocessors is common and does not turn a single-processor system into a multiprocessor. If there is only one general-purpose CPU, then the system is a single-processor system.

1.3.2 Multiprocessor Systems

Although single-processor systems are most common, **multiprocessor systems** (also known as **parallel systems** or **tightly coupled systems**) are growing in importance. Such systems have two or more processors in close communication, sharing the computer bus and sometimes the clock, memory, and peripheral devices.

Multiprocessor systems have three main advantages:

1. **Increased throughput**. By increasing the number of processors, we expect to get more work done in less time. The speed-up ratio with N processors is not N, however; rather, it is less than N. When multiple processors cooperate on a task, a certain amount of overhead is incurred in keeping all the parts working correctly. This overhead, plus contention for shared resources, lowers the expected gain from additional processors. Similarly, N programmers working closely together do not produce N times the amount of work a single programmer would produce.

2. **Economy of scale**. Multiprocessor systems can cost less than equivalent multiple single-processor systems, because they can share peripherals, mass storage, and power supplies. If several programs operate on the same set of data, it is cheaper to store those data on one disk and to have all the processors share them than to have many computers with local disks and many copies of the data.

3. **Increased reliability**. If functions can be distributed properly among several processors, then the failure of one processor will not halt the system, only slow it down. If we have ten processors and one fails, then each of the remaining nine processors can pick up a share of the work of the failed processor. Thus, the entire system runs only 10 percent slower, rather than failing altogether.

Increased reliability of a computer system is crucial in many applications. The ability to continue providing service proportional to the level of surviving hardware is called graceful degradation. Some systems go beyond graceful degradation and are called fault tolerant, because they can suffer a failure of any single component and still continue operation. Note that fault tolerance requires a mechanism to allow the failure to be detected, diagnosed, and, if possible, corrected. The HP NonStop (formerly Tandem) system uses both hardware and software duplication to ensure continued operation despite faults. The system consists of multiple pairs of CPUs, working in lockstep. Both processors in the pair execute each instruction and compare the results. If the results differ, then one CPU of the pair is at fault, and both are halted. The process that was being executed is then moved to another pair of CPUs, and the instruction that failed is restarted. This solution is expensive, since it involves special hardware and considerable hardware duplication.

The multiple-processor systems in use today are of two types. Some systems use asymmetric multiprocessing, in which each processor is assigned a specific task. A master processor controls the system; the other processors either look to the master for instruction or have predefined tasks. This scheme defines a master–slave relationship. The master processor schedules and allocates work to the slave processors.

The most common systems use symmetric multiprocessing (SMP), in which each processor performs all tasks within the operating system. SMP means that all processors are peers; no master–slave relationship exists between processors. Figure 1.6 illustrates a typical SMP architecture. Notice that each processor has its own set of registers, as well as a private—or local— cache; however, all processors share physical memory. An example of the SMP system is Solaris, a commercial version of UNIX designed by Sun Microsystems. A Solaris system can be configured to employ dozens of processors, all running

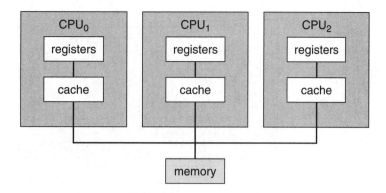

Figure 1.6 Symmetric multiprocessing architecture.

Solaris. The benefit of this model is that many processes can run simultaneously —N processes can run if there are N CPUs—without causing a significant deterioration of performance. However, we must carefully control I/O to ensure that the data reach the appropriate processor. Also, since the CPUs are separate, one may be sitting idle while another is overloaded, resulting in inefficiencies. These inefficiencies can be avoided if the processors share certain data structures. A multiprocessor system of this form will allow processes and resources—such as memory—to be shared dynamically among the various processors and can lower the variance among the processors. Such a system must be written carefully, as we shall see in Chapter 6. Virtually all modern operating systems—including Windows, Windows XP, Mac OS X, and Linux—now provide support for SMP.

The difference between symmetric and asymmetric multiprocessing may result from either hardware or software. Special hardware can differentiate the multiple processors, or the software can be written to allow only one master and multiple slaves. For instance, Sun's operating system SunOS Version 4 provided asymmetric multiprocessing, whereas Version 5 (Solaris) is symmetric on the same hardware.

Multiprocessing adds CPUs to increase computing power. If the CPU has an integrated memory controller, then adding CPUs can also increase the amount of memory addressable in the system. Either way, multiprocessing can cause a system to change its memory access model from uniform memory access (UMA) to non-uniform memory access (NUMA). UMA is defined as the situation in which access to any RAM from any CPU takes the same amount of time. With NUMA, some parts of memory may take longer to access than other parts, creating a performance penalty. Operating systems can minimize the NUMA penalty through resource management, as discussed in Section 9.5.4.

A recent trend in CPU design is to include multiple computing cores on a single chip. In essence, these are multiprocessor chips. They can be more efficient than multiple chips with single cores because on-chip communication is faster than between-chip communication. In addition, one chip with multiple cores uses significantly less power than multiple single-core chips. As a result, multicore systems are especially well suited for server systems such as database and Web servers.

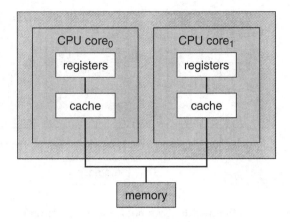

Figure 1.7 A dual-core design with two cores placed on the same chip.

In Figure 1.7, we show a dual-core design with two cores on the same chip. In this design, each core has its own register set as well as its own local cache; other designs might use a shared cache or a combination of local and shared caches. Aside from architectural considerations, such as cache, memory, and bus contention, these multicore CPUs appear to the operating system as N standard processors. This tendency puts pressure on operating system designers—and application programmers—to make use of those CPUs.

Finally, **blade servers** are a recent development in which multiple processor boards, I/O boards, and networking boards are placed in the same chassis. The difference between these and traditional multiprocessor systems is that each blade-processor board boots independently and runs its own operating system. Some blade-server boards are multiprocessor as well, which blurs the lines between types of computers. In essence, these servers consist of multiple independent multiprocessor systems.

1.3.3 Clustered Systems

Another type of multiple-CPU system is the **clustered system**. Like multiprocessor systems, clustered systems gather together multiple CPUs to accomplish computational work. Clustered systems differ from multiprocessor systems, however, in that they are composed of two or more individual systems—or nodes—joined together. The definition of the term *clustered* is not concrete; many commercial packages wrestle with what a clustered system is and why one form is better than another. The generally accepted definition is that clustered computers share storage and are closely linked via a **local-area network (LAN)** (as described in Section 1.10) or a faster interconnect, such as InfiniBand.

Clustering is usually used to provide **high-availability** service; that is, service will continue even if one or more systems in the cluster fail. High availability is generally obtained by adding a level of redundancy in the system. A layer of cluster software runs on the cluster nodes. Each node can monitor one or more of the others (over the LAN). If the monitored machine fails, the monitoring machine can take ownership of its storage and restart the applications that were running on the failed machine. The users and clients of the applications see only a brief interruption of service.

BEOWULF CLUSTERS

Beowulf clusters are designed for solving high-performance computing tasks. These clusters are built using commodity hardware—such as personal computers—that are connected via a simple local area network. Interestingly, a Beowulf cluster uses no one specific software package but rather consists of a set of open-source software libraries that allow the computing nodes in the cluster to communicate with one another. Thus, there are a variety of approaches for constructing a Beowulf cluster, although Beowulf computing nodes typically run the Linux operating system. Since Beowulf clusters require no special hardware and operate using open-source software that is freely available, they offer a low-cost strategy for building a high-performance computing cluster. In fact, some Beowulf clusters built from collections of discarded personal computers are using hundreds of computing nodes to solve computationally expensive problems in scientific computing.

Clustering can be structured asymmetrically or symmetrically. In **asymmetric clustering**, one machine is in **hot-standby mode** while the other is running the applications. The hot-standby host machine does nothing but monitor the active server. If that server fails, the hot-standby host becomes the active server. In **symmetric mode**, two or more hosts are running applications and are monitoring each other. This mode is obviously more efficient, as it uses all of the available hardware. It does require that more than one application be available to run.

As a cluster consists of several computer systems connected via a network, clusters may also be used to provide **high-performance computing** environments. Such systems can supply significantly greater computational power than single-processor or even SMP systems because they are capable of running an application concurrently on all computers in the cluster. However, applications must be written specifically to take advantage of the cluster by using a technique known as **parallelization**, which consists of dividing a program into separate components that run in parallel on individual computers in the cluster. Typically, these applications are designed so that once each computing node in the cluster has solved its portion of the problem, the results from all the nodes are combined into a final solution.

Other forms of clusters include parallel clusters and clustering over a wide-area network (WAN) (as described in Section 1.10). Parallel clusters allow multiple hosts to access the same data on the shared storage. Because most operating systems lack support for simultaneous data access by multiple hosts, parallel clusters are usually accomplished by use of special versions of software and special releases of applications. For example, Oracle Real Application Cluster is a version of Oracle's database that has been designed to run on a parallel cluster. Each machine runs Oracle, and a layer of software tracks access to the shared disk. Each machine has full access to all data in the database. To provide this shared access to data, the system must also supply access control and locking to ensure that no conflicting operations occur. This function, commonly known as a **distributed lock manager (DLM)**, is included in some cluster technology.

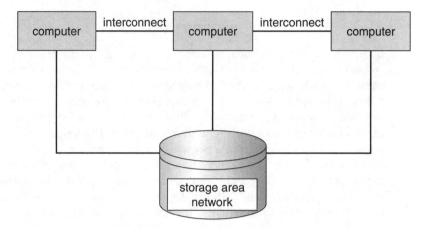

Figure 1.8   General structure of a clustered system.

Cluster technology is changing rapidly. Some cluster products support dozens of systems in a cluster, as well as clustered nodes that are separated by miles. Many of these improvements are made possible by **storage-area networks (SANs)**, as described in Section 12.3.3, which allow many systems to attach to a pool of storage. If the applications and their data are stored on the SAN, then the cluster software can assign the application to run on any host that is attached to the SAN. If the host fails, then any other host can take over. In a database cluster, dozens of hosts can share the same database, greatly increasing performance and reliability. Figure 1.8 depicts the general structure of a clustered system.

1.4   Operating-System Structure

Now that we have discussed basic information about computer-system orga-nization and architecture, we are ready to talk about operating systems. An operating system provides the environment within which programs are executed. Internally, operating systems vary greatly in their makeup, since they are organized along many different lines. There are, however, many commonalities, which we consider in this section.

One of the most important aspects of operating systems is the ability to multiprogram. A single program cannot, in general, keep either the CPU or the I/O devices busy at all times. Single users frequently have multiple programs running. **Multiprogramming** increases CPU utilization by organizing jobs (code and data) so that the CPU always has one to execute.

The idea is as follows: The operating system keeps several jobs in memory simultaneously (Figure 1.9). Since, in general, main memory is too small to accommodate all jobs, the jobs are kept initially on the disk in the **job pool**. This pool consists of all processes residing on disk awaiting allocation of main memory.

The set of jobs in memory can be a subset of the jobs kept in the job pool. The operating system picks and begins to execute one of the jobs in memory. Eventually, the job may have to wait for some task, such as an I/O operation,

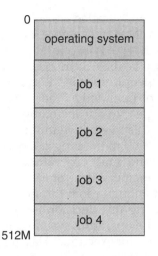

Figure 1.9 Memory layout for a multiprogramming system.

to complete. In a non-multiprogrammed system, the CPU would sit idle. In a multiprogrammed system, the operating system simply switches to, and executes, another job. When *that* job needs to wait, the CPU is switched to *another* job, and so on. Eventually, the first job finishes waiting and gets the CPU back. As long as at least one job needs to execute, the CPU is never idle.

This idea is common in other life situations. A lawyer does not work for only one client at a time, for example. While one case is waiting to go to trial or have papers typed, the lawyer can work on another case. If he has enough clients, the lawyer will never be idle for lack of work. (Idle lawyers tend to become politicians, so there is a certain social value in keeping lawyers busy.)

Multiprogrammed systems provide an environment in which the various system resources (for example, CPU, memory, and peripheral devices) are utilized effectively, but they do not provide for user interaction with the computer system. **Time sharing** (or **multitasking**) is a logical extension of multiprogramming. In time-sharing systems, the CPU executes multiple jobs by switching among them, but the switches occur so frequently that the users can interact with each program while it is running.

Time sharing requires an **interactive** (or **hands-on**) **computer system**, which provides direct communication between the user and the system. The user gives instructions to the operating system or to a program directly, using an input device such as a keyboard or a mouse, and waits for immediate results on an output device. Accordingly, the **response time** should be short—typically less than one second.

A time-shared operating system allows many users to share the computer simultaneously. Since each action or command in a time-shared system tends to be short, only a little CPU time is needed for each user. As the system switches rapidly from one user to the next, each user is given the impression that the entire computer system is dedicated to his use, even though it is being shared among many users.

A time-shared operating system uses CPU scheduling and multiprogramming to provide each user with a small portion of a time-shared computer. Each user has at least one separate program in memory. A program loaded into memory and executing is called a process. When a process executes, it typically executes for only a short time before it either finishes or needs to perform I/O. I/O may be interactive; that is, output goes to a display for the user, and input comes from a user keyboard, mouse, or other device. Since interactive I/O typically runs at "people speeds," it may take a long time to complete. Input, for example, may be bounded by the user's typing speed; seven characters per second is fast for people but incredibly slow for computers. Rather than let the CPU sit idle as this interactive input takes place, the operating system will rapidly switch the CPU to the program of some other user.

Time sharing and multiprogramming require that several jobs be kept simultaneously in memory. If several jobs are ready to be brought into memory, and if there is not enough room for all of them, then the system must choose among them. Making this decision is job scheduling, which is discussed in Chapter 5. When the operating system selects a job from the job pool, it loads that job into memory for execution. Having several programs in memory at the same time requires some form of memory management, which is covered in Chapters 8 and 9. In addition, if several jobs are ready to run at the same time, the system must choose among them. Making this decision is CPU scheduling, which is discussed in Chapter 5. Finally, running multiple jobs concurrently requires that their ability to affect one another be limited in all phases of the operating system, including process scheduling, disk storage, and memory management. These considerations are discussed throughout the text.

In a time-sharing system, the operating system must ensure reasonable response time, which is sometimes accomplished through swapping, where processes are swapped in and out of main memory to the disk. A more common method for achieving this goal is virtual memory, a technique that allows the execution of a process that is not completely in memory (Chapter 9). The main advantage of the virtual-memory scheme is that it enables users to run programs that are larger than actual physical memory. Further, it abstracts main memory into a large, uniform array of storage, separating logical memory as viewed by the user from physical memory. This arrangement frees programmers from concern over memory-storage limitations.

Time-sharing systems must also provide a file system (Chapters 10 and 11). The file system resides on a collection of disks; hence, disk management must be provided (Chapter 12). Also, time-sharing systems provide a mechanism for protecting resources from inappropriate use (Chapter 14). To ensure orderly execution, the system must provide mechanisms for job synchronization and communication (Chapter 6), and it may ensure that jobs do not get stuck in a deadlock, forever waiting for one another (Chapter 7).

1.5 Operating-System Operations

As mentioned earlier, modern operating systems are interrupt driven. If there are no processes to execute, no I/O devices to service, and no users to whom to respond, an operating system will sit quietly, waiting for something to happen. Events are almost always signaled by the occurrence of an interrupt or a trap. A trap (or an exception) is a software-generated interrupt caused either by an error (for example, division by zero or invalid memory access) or by a specific request from a user program that an operating-system service be performed. The interrupt-driven nature of an operating system defines that system's general structure. For each type of interrupt, separate segments of code in the operating system determine what action should be taken. An interrupt service routine is provided that is responsible for dealing with the interrupt.

Since the operating system and the users share the hardware and software resources of the computer system, we need to make sure that an error in a user program could cause problems only for the one program running. With sharing, many processes could be adversely affected by a bug in one program. For example, if a process gets stuck in an infinite loop, this loop could prevent the correct operation of many other processes. More subtle errors can occur in a multiprogramming system, where one erroneous program might modify another program, the data of another program, or even the operating system itself.

Without protection against these sorts of errors, either the computer must execute only one process at a time or all output must be suspect. A properly designed operating system must ensure that an incorrect (or malicious) program cannot cause other programs to execute incorrectly.

1.5.1 Dual-Mode Operation

In order to ensure the proper execution of the operating system, we must be able to distinguish between the execution of operating-system code and user-defined code. The approach taken by most computer systems is to provide hardware support that allows us to differentiate among various modes of execution.

At the very least, we need two separate modes of operation: user mode and kernel mode (also called supervisor mode, system mode, or privileged mode). A bit, called the mode bit, is added to the hardware of the computer to indicate the current mode: kernel (0) or user (1). With the mode bit, we are able to distinguish between a task that is executed on behalf of the operating system and one that is executed on behalf of the user. When the computer system is executing on behalf of a user application, the system is in user mode. However, when a user application requests a service from the operating system (via a system call), it must transition from user to kernel mode to fulfill the request. This is shown in Figure 1.10. As we shall see, this architectural enhancement is useful for many other aspects of system operation as well.

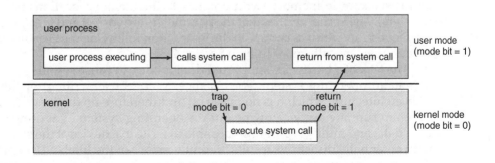

Figure 1.10   Transition from user to kernel mode.

At system boot time, the hardware starts in kernel mode. The operating system is then loaded and starts user applications in user mode. Whenever a trap or interrupt occurs, the hardware switches from user mode to kernel mode (that is, changes the state of the mode bit to 0). Thus, whenever the operating system gains control of the computer, it is in kernel mode. The system always switches to user mode (by setting the mode bit to 1) before passing control to a user program.

The dual mode of operation provides us with the means for protecting the operating system from errant users—and errant users from one another. We accomplish this protection by designating some of the machine instructions that may cause harm as **privileged instructions**. The hardware allows privileged instructions to be executed only in kernel mode. If an attempt is made to execute a privileged instruction in user mode, the hardware does not execute the instruction but rather treats it as illegal and traps it to the operating system.

The instruction to switch to kernel mode is an example of a privileged instruction. Some other examples include I/O control, timer management, and interrupt management. As we shall see throughout the text, there are many additional privileged instructions.

We can now see the life cycle of instruction execution in a computer system. Initial control resides in the operating system, where instructions are executed in kernel mode. When control is given to a user application, the mode is set to user mode. Eventually, control is switched back to the operating system via an interrupt, a trap, or a system call.

System calls provide the means for a user program to ask the operating system to perform tasks reserved for the operating system on the user program's behalf. A system call is invoked in a variety of ways, depending on the functionality provided by the underlying processor. In all forms, it is the method used by a process to request action by the operating system. A system call usually takes the form of a trap to a specific location in the interrupt vector. This trap can be executed by a generic `trap` instruction, although some systems (such as the MIPS R2000 family) have a specific `syscall` instruction.

When a system call is executed, it is treated by the hardware as a software interrupt. Control passes through the interrupt vector to a service routine in the operating system, and the mode bit is set to kernel mode. The system-call service routine is a part of the operating system. The kernel examines the interrupting instruction to determine what system call has occurred; a parameter indicates what type of service the user program is requesting. Additional information needed for the request may be passed in registers, on the stack, or in memory (with pointers to the memory locations passed in registers). The kernel verifies that the parameters are correct and legal, executes the request, and returns control to the instruction following the system call. We describe system calls more fully in Section 2.3.

The lack of a hardware-supported dual mode can cause serious shortcomings in an operating system. For instance, MS-DOS was written for the Intel 8088 architecture, which has no mode bit and therefore no dual mode. A user program running awry can wipe out the operating system by writing over it with data; and multiple programs are able to write to a device at the same time, with potentially disastrous results. Recent versions of the Intel CPU do provide dual-mode operation. Accordingly, most contemporary operating systems—such as Microsoft Vista and Windows XP, as well as Unix, Linux, and Solaris

—take advantage of this dual-mode feature and provide greater protection for the operating system.

Once hardware protection is in place, it detects errors that violate modes. These errors are normally handled by the operating system. If a user program fails in some way—such as by making an attempt either to execute an illegal instruction or to access memory that is not in the user's address space—then the hardware traps to the operating system. The trap transfers control through the interrupt vector to the operating system, just as an interrupt does. When a program error occurs, the operating system must terminate the program abnormally. This situation is handled by the same code as a user-requested abnormal termination. An appropriate error message is given, and the memory of the program may be dumped. The memory dump is usually written to a file so that the user or programmer can examine it and perhaps correct it and restart the program.

1.5.2 Timer

We must ensure that the operating system maintains control over the CPU. We cannot allow a user program to get stuck in an infinite loop or to fail to call system services and never return control to the operating system. To accomplish this goal, we can use a **timer**. A timer can be set to interrupt the computer after a specified period. The period may be fixed (for example, 1/60 second) or variable (for example, from 1 millisecond to 1 second). A **variable timer** is generally implemented by a fixed-rate clock and a counter. The operating system sets the counter. Every time the clock ticks, the counter is decremented. When the counter reaches 0, an interrupt occurs. For instance, a 10-bit counter with a 1-millisecond clock allows interrupts at intervals from 1 millisecond to 1,024 milliseconds, in steps of 1 millisecond.

Before turning over control to the user, the operating system ensures that the timer is set to interrupt. If the timer interrupts, control transfers automatically to the operating system, which may treat the interrupt as a fatal error or may give the program more time. Clearly, instructions that modify the content of the timer are privileged.

Thus, we can use the timer to prevent a user program from running too long. A simple technique is to initialize a counter with the amount of time that a program is allowed to run. A program with a 7-minute time limit, for example, would have its counter initialized to 420. Every second, the timer interrupts and the counter is decremented by 1. As long as the counter is positive, control is returned to the user program. When the counter becomes negative, the operating system terminates the program for exceeding the assigned time limit.

1.6 Process Management

A program does nothing unless its instructions are executed by a CPU. A program in execution, as mentioned, is a process. A time-shared user program such as a compiler is a process. A word-processing program being run by an individual user on a PC is a process. A system task, such as sending output to a printer, can also be a process (or at least part of one). For now, you can consider a process to be a job or a time-shared program, but later you will learn that the concept is more general. As we shall see in Chapter 3, it is possible to provide system calls that allow processes to create subprocesses to execute concurrently.

A process needs certain resources—including CPU time, memory, files, and I/O devices—to accomplish its task. These resources are either given to the process when it is created or allocated to it while it is running. In addition to the various physical and logical resources that a process obtains when it is created, various initialization data (input) may be passed along. For example, consider a process whose function is to display the status of a file on the screen of a terminal. The process will be given as an input the name of the file and will execute the appropriate instructions and system calls to obtain and display on the terminal the desired information. When the process terminates, the operating system will reclaim any reusable resources.

We emphasize that a program by itself is not a process; a program is a *passive* entity, like the contents of a file stored on disk, whereas a process is an *active* entity. A single-threaded process has one **program counter** specifying the next instruction to execute. (Threads are covered in Chapter 4.) The execution of such a process must be sequential. The CPU executes one instruction of the process after another, until the process completes. Further, at any time, one instruction at most is executed on behalf of the process. Thus, although two processes may be associated with the same program, they are nevertheless considered two separate execution sequences. A multithreaded process has multiple program counters, each pointing to the next instruction to execute for a given thread.

A process is the unit of work in a system. Such a system consists of a collection of processes, some of which are operating-system processes (those that execute system code) and the rest of which are user processes (those that execute user code). All these processes can potentially execute concurrently— by multiplexing on a single CPU, for example.

The operating system is responsible for the following activities in connection with process management:

- Scheduling processes and threads on the CPUs
- Creating and deleting both user and system processes
- Suspending and resuming processes
- Providing mechanisms for process synchronization
- Providing mechanisms for process communication

We discuss process-management techniques in Chapters 3 through 6.

1.7   Memory Management

As we discussed in Section 1.2.2, the main memory is central to the operation of a modern computer system. Main memory is a large array of words or bytes, ranging in size from hundreds of thousands to billions. Each word or byte has its own address. Main memory is a repository of quickly accessible data shared by the CPU and I/O devices. The central processor reads instructions from main memory during the instruction-fetch cycle and both reads and writes data from main memory during the data-fetch cycle (on a von Neumann architecture). As noted earlier, the main memory is generally the only large storage device that the CPU is able to address and access directly. For example, for the CPU to process data from disk, those data must first be transferred to main memory by CPU-generated I/O calls. In the same way, instructions must be in memory for the CPU to execute them.

For a program to be executed, it must be mapped to absolute addresses and loaded into memory. As the program executes, it accesses program instructions and data from memory by generating these absolute addresses. Eventually, the program terminates, its memory space is declared available, and the next program can be loaded and executed.

To improve both the utilization of the CPU and the speed of the computer's response to its users, general-purpose computers must keep several programs in memory, creating a need for memory management. Many different memory-management schemes are used. These schemes reflect various approaches, and the effectiveness of any given algorithm depends on the situation. In selecting a memory-management scheme for a specific system, we must take into account many factors—especially the *hardware* design of the system. Each algorithm requires its own hardware support.

The operating system is responsible for the following activities in connection with memory management:

- Keeping track of which parts of memory are currently being used and by whom

- Deciding which processes (or parts thereof) and data to move into and out of memory

- Allocating and deallocating memory space as needed

Memory-management techniques are discussed in Chapters 8 and 9.

1.8 Storage Management

To make the computer system convenient for users, the operating system provides a uniform, logical view of information storage. The operating system abstracts from the physical properties of its storage devices to define a logical storage unit, the file. The operating system maps files onto physical media and accesses these files via the storage devices.

1.8.1 File-System Management

File management is one of the most visible components of an operating system. Computers can store information on several different types of physical media. Magnetic disk, optical disk, and magnetic tape are the most common. Each of these media has its own characteristics and physical organization. Each medium is controlled by a device, such as a disk drive or tape drive, that also has its own unique characteristics. These properties include access speed, capacity, data-transfer rate, and access method (sequential or random).

A file is a collection of related information defined by its creator. Commonly, files represent programs (both source and object forms) and data. Data files may be numeric, alphabetic, alphanumeric, or binary. Files may be free-form (for example, text files), or they may be formatted rigidly (for example, fixed fields). Clearly, the concept of a file is an extremely general one.

The operating system implements the abstract concept of a file by managing mass-storage media, such as tapes and disks, and the devices that control them. Also, files are normally organized into directories to make them easier to use. Finally, when multiple users have access to files, it may be desirable to control by whom and in what ways (for example, read, write, append) files may be accessed.

The operating system is responsible for the following activities in connection with file management:

- Creating and deleting files

- Creating and deleting directories to organize files

- Supporting primitives for manipulating files and directories

- Mapping files onto secondary storage

- Backing up files on stable (nonvolatile) storage media

File-management techniques are discussed in Chapters 10 and 11.

1.8.2   Mass-Storage Management

As we have already seen, because main memory is too small to accommodate all data and programs, and because the data that it holds are lost when power is lost, the computer system must provide secondary storage to back up main memory. Most modern computer systems use disks as the principal on-line storage medium for both programs and data. Most programs—including compilers, assemblers, word processors, editors, and formatters—are stored on a disk until loaded into memory and then use the disk as both the source and destination of their processing. Hence, the proper management of disk storage is of central importance to a computer system. The operating system is responsible for the following activities in connection with disk management:

- Free-space management

- Storage allocation

- Disk scheduling

Because secondary storage is used frequently, it must be used efficiently. The entire speed of operation of a computer may hinge on the speeds of the disk subsystem and the algorithms that manipulate that subsystem.

There are, however, many uses for storage that is slower and lower in cost (and sometimes of higher capacity) than secondary storage. Backups of disk data, seldom-used data, and long-term archival storage are some examples. Magnetic tape drives and their tapes and CD and DVD drives and platters are typical **tertiary storage** devices. The media (tapes and optical platters) vary between WORM (write-once, read-many-times) and RW (read–write) formats.

Tertiary storage is not crucial to system performance, but it still must be managed. Some operating systems take on this task, while others leave tertiary-storage management to application programs. Some of the functions that operating systems can provide include mounting and unmounting media in devices, allocating and freeing the devices for exclusive use by processes, and migrating data from secondary to tertiary storage.

Techniques for secondary and tertiary storage management are discussed in Chapter 12.

1.8.3 Caching

Caching is an important principle of computer systems. Information is normally kept in some storage system (such as main memory). As it is used, it is copied into a faster storage system—the cache—on a temporary basis. When we need a particular piece of information, we first check whether it is in the cache. If it is, we use the information directly from the cache; if it is not, we use the information from the source, putting a copy in the cache under the assumption that we will need it again soon.

In addition, internal programmable registers, such as index registers, provide a high-speed cache for main memory. The programmer (or compiler) implements the register-allocation and register-replacement algorithms to decide which information to keep in registers and which to keep in main memory. There are also caches that are implemented totally in hardware. For instance, most systems have an instruction cache to hold the instructions expected to be executed next. Without this cache, the CPU would have to wait several cycles while an instruction was fetched from main memory. For similar reasons, most systems have one or more high-speed data caches in the memory hierarchy. We are not concerned with these hardware-only caches in this text, since they are outside the control of the operating system.

Because caches have limited size, cache management is an important design problem. Careful selection of the cache size and of a replacement policy can result in greatly increased performance. Figure 1.11 compares storage performance in large workstations and small servers. Various replacement algorithms for software-controlled caches are discussed in Chapter 9.

Level	1	2	3	4
Name	registers	cache	main memory	disk storage
Typical size	< 1 KB	< 16 MB	< 64 GB	> 100 GB
Implementation technology	custom memory with multiple ports, CMOS	on-chip or off-chip CMOS SRAM	CMOS DRAM	magnetic disk
Access time (ns)	0.25 – 0.5	0.5 – 25	80 – 250	5,000.000
Bandwidth (MB/sec)	20,000 – 100,000	5000 – 10,000	1000 – 5000	20 – 150
Managed by	compiler	hardware	operating system	operating system
Backed by	cache	main memory	disk	CD or tape

Figure 1.11 Performance of various levels of storage.

Main memory can be viewed as a fast cache for secondary storage, since data in secondary storage must be copied into main memory for use, and data must be in main memory before being moved to secondary storage for safekeeping. The file-system data, which resides permanently on secondary storage, may appear on several levels in the storage hierarchy. At the highest level, the operating system may maintain a cache of file-system data in main memory. In addition, electronic RAM disks (also known as **solid-state disks**) may be used for high-speed storage that is accessed through the file-system interface. The bulk of secondary storage is on magnetic disks. The magnetic-disk storage, in turn, is often backed up onto magnetic tapes or removable disks to protect against data loss in case of a hard-disk failure. Some systems automatically archive old file data from secondary storage to tertiary storage, such as tape jukeboxes, to lower the storage cost (see Chapter 12).

The movement of information between levels of a storage hierarchy may be either explicit or implicit, depending on the hardware design and the controlling operating-system software. For instance, data transfer from cache to CPU and registers is usually a hardware function, with no operating-system intervention. In contrast, transfer of data from disk to memory is usually controlled by the operating system.

In a hierarchical storage structure, the same data may appear in different levels of the storage system. For example, suppose that an integer A that is to be incremented by 1 is located in file B, and file B resides on magnetic disk. The increment operation proceeds by first issuing an I/O operation to copy the disk block on which A resides to main memory. This operation is followed by copying A to the cache and to an internal register. Thus, the copy of A appears in several places: on the magnetic disk, in main memory, in the cache, and in an internal register (see Figure 1.12). Once the increment takes place in the internal register, the value of A differs in the various storage systems. The value of A becomes the same only after the new value of A is written from the internal register back to the magnetic disk.

In a computing environment where only one process executes at a time, this arrangement poses no difficulties, since an access to integer A will always be to the copy at the highest level of the hierarchy. However, in a multitasking environment, where the CPU is switched back and forth among various processes, extreme care must be taken to ensure that, if several processes wish to access A, then each of these processes will obtain the most recently updated value of A.

The situation becomes more complicated in a multiprocessor environment where, in addition to maintaining internal registers, each of the CPUs also contains a local cache (Figure 1.6). In such an environment, a copy of A may exist simultaneously in several caches. Since the various CPUs can all execute concurrently, we must make sure that an update to the value of A in one cache

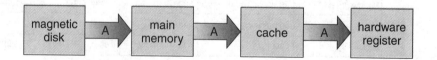

Figure 1.12   Migration of integer A from disk to register.

is immediately reflected in all other caches where A resides. This situation is called **cache coherency**, and it is usually a hardware problem (handled below the operating-system level).

In a distributed environment, the situation becomes even more complex. In this environment, several copies (or replicas) of the same file can be kept on different computers that are distributed in space. Since the various replicas may be accessed and updated concurrently, some distributed systems ensure that, when a replica is updated in one place, all other replicas are brought up to date as soon as possible. There are various ways to achieve this guarantee, as we discuss in Chapter 17.

1.8.4 I/O Systems

One of the purposes of an operating system is to hide the peculiarities of specific hardware devices from the user. For example, in UNIX, the peculiarities of I/O devices are hidden from the bulk of the operating system itself by the **I/O subsystem**. The I/O subsystem consists of several components:

- A memory-management component that includes buffering, caching, and spooling
- A general device-driver interface
- Drivers for specific hardware devices

Only the device driver knows the peculiarities of the specific device to which it is assigned.

We discussed in Section 1.2.3 how interrupt handlers and device drivers are used in the construction of efficient I/O subsystems. In Chapter 13, we discuss how the I/O subsystem interfaces to the other system components, manages devices, transfers data, and detects I/O completion.

1.9 Protection and Security

If a computer system has multiple users and allows the concurrent execution of multiple processes, then access to data must be regulated. For that purpose, mechanisms ensure that files, memory segments, CPU, and other resources can be operated on by only those processes that have gained proper authorization from the operating system. For example, memory-addressing hardware ensures that a process can execute only within its own address space. The timer ensures that no process can gain control of the CPU without eventually relinquishing control. Device-control registers are not accessible to users, so the integrity of the various peripheral devices is protected.

Protection, then, is any mechanism for controlling the access of processes or users to the resources defined by a computer system. This mechanism must provide means to specify the controls to be imposed and means to enforce the controls.

Protection can improve reliability by detecting latent errors at the interfaces between component subsystems. Early detection of interface errors can often prevent contamination of a healthy subsystem by another subsystem that is malfunctioning. Furthermore, an unprotected resource cannot defend against use (or misuse) by an unauthorized or incompetent user. A protection-oriented system provides a means to distinguish between authorized and unauthorized usage, as we discuss in Chapter 14.

A system can have adequate protection but still be prone to failure and allow inappropriate access. Consider a user whose authentication information (her means of identifying herself to the system) is stolen. Her data could be copied or deleted, even though file and memory protection are working. It is the job of **security** to defend a system from external and internal attacks. Such attacks spread across a huge range and include viruses and worms, denial-of-service attacks (which use all of a system's resources and so keep legitimate users out of the system), identity theft, and theft of service (unauthorized use of a system). Prevention of some of these attacks is considered an operating-system function on some systems, while other systems leave the prevention to policy or additional software. Due to the alarming rise in security incidents, operating-system security features represent a fast-growing area of research and implementation. Security is discussed in Chapter 15.

Protection and security require the system to be able to distinguish among all its users. Most operating systems maintain a list of user names and associated **user identifiers (user IDs)**. In Windows Vista parlance, this is a **security ID (SID)**. These numerical IDs are unique, one per user. When a user logs in to the system, the authentication stage determines the appropriate user ID for the user. That user ID is associated with all of the user's processes and threads. When an ID needs to be user readable, it is translated back to the user name via the user name list.

In some circumstances, we wish to distinguish among sets of users rather than individual users. For example, the owner of a file on a UNIX system may be allowed to issue all operations on that file, whereas a selected set of users may only be allowed to read the file. To accomplish this, we need to define a group name and the set of users belonging to that group. Group functionality can be implemented as a system-wide list of group names and **group identifiers**. A user can be in one or more groups, depending on operating-system design decisions. The user's group IDs are also included in every associated process and thread.

In the course of normal use of a system, the user ID and group ID for a user are sufficient. However, a user sometimes needs to **escalate privileges** to gain extra permissions for an activity. The user may need access to a device that is restricted, for example. Operating systems provide various methods to allow privilege escalation. On UNIX, for example, the `setuid` attribute on a program causes that program to run with the user ID of the owner of the file, rather than the current user's ID. The process runs with this **effective UID** until it turns off the extra privileges or terminates.

1.10   Distributed Systems

A distributed system is a collection of physically separate, possibly heterogeneous, computer systems that are networked to provide the users with access to the various resources that the system maintains. Access to a shared resource increases computation speed, functionality, data availability, and reliability. Some operating systems generalize network access as a form of file access, with the details of networking contained in the network interface's device driver. Others make users specifically invoke network functions. Generally, systems contain a mix of the two modes—for example FTP and NFS. The protocols that create a distributed system can greatly affect that system's utility and popularity.

A **network**, in the simplest terms, is a communication path between two or more systems. Distributed systems depend on networking for their functionality. Networks vary by the protocols used, the distances between nodes, and the transport media. TCP/IP is the most common network protocol, although ATM and other protocols are in widespread use. Likewise, operating-system support of protocols varies. Most operating systems support TCP/IP, including the Windows and UNIX operating systems. Some systems support proprietary protocols to suit their needs. To an operating system, a network protocol simply needs an interface device—a network adapter, for example— with a device driver to manage it, as well as software to handle data. These concepts are discussed throughout this book.

Networks are characterized based on the distances between their nodes. A **local-area network (LAN)** connects computers within a room, a floor, or a building. A **wide-area network (WAN)** usually links buildings, cities, or countries. A global company may have a WAN to connect its offices worldwide. These networks may run one protocol or several protocols. The continuing advent of new technologies brings about new forms of networks. For example, a **metropolitan-area network (MAN)** could link buildings within a city. BlueTooth and 802.11 devices use wireless technology to communicate over a distance of several feet, in essence creating a **small-area network** such as might be found in a home.

The media to carry networks are equally varied. They include copper wires, fiber strands, and wireless transmissions between satellites, microwave dishes, and radios. When computing devices are connected to cellular phones, they create a network. Even very short-range infrared communication can be used for networking. At a rudimentary level, whenever computers communicate, they use or create a network. These networks also vary in their performance and reliability.

Some operating systems have taken the concept of networks and distributed systems further than the notion of providing network connectivity. A **network operating system** is an operating system that provides features such as file sharing across the network and that includes a communication scheme that allows different processes on different computers to exchange messages. A computer running a network operating system acts autonomously from all other computers on the network, although it is aware of the network and is able to communicate with other networked computers. A distributed operating system provides a less autonomous environment: The different operating systems communicate closely enough to provide the illusion that only a single operating system controls the network.

We cover computer networks and distributed systems in Chapters 16 through 18.

1.11 Special-Purpose Systems

The discussion thus far has focused on the general-purpose computer systems that we are all familiar with. There are, however, other classes of computer systems whose functions are more limited and whose objective is to deal with limited computation domains.

1.11.1 Real-Time Embedded Systems

Embedded computers are the most prevalent form of computers in existence. These devices are found everywhere, from car engines and manufacturing robots to DVDs and microwave ovens. They tend to have very specific tasks. The systems they run on are usually primitive, and so the operating systems provide limited features. Usually, they have little or no user interface, preferring to spend their time monitoring and managing hardware devices, such as automobile engines and robotic arms.

These embedded systems vary considerably. Some are general-purpose computers, running standard operating systems—such as UNIX—with special-purpose applications to implement the functionality. Others are hardware devices with a special-purpose embedded operating system providing just the functionality desired. Yet others are hardware devices with application-specific integrated circuits (ASICs) that perform their tasks without an operating system.

The use of embedded systems continues to expand. The power of these devices, both as standalone units and as elements of networks and the Web, is sure to increase as well. Even now, entire houses can be computerized, so that a central computer—either a general-purpose computer or an embedded system—can control heating and lighting, alarm systems, and even coffee makers. Web access can enable a home owner to tell the house to heat up before she arrives home. Someday, the refrigerator may call the grocery store when it notices the milk is gone.

Embedded systems almost always run **real-time operating systems**. A real-time system is used when rigid time requirements have been placed on the operation of a processor or the flow of data; thus, it is often used as a control device in a dedicated application. Sensors bring data to the computer. The computer must analyze the data and possibly adjust controls to modify the sensor inputs. Systems that control scientific experiments, medical imaging systems, industrial control systems, and certain display systems are real-time systems. Some automobile-engine fuel-injection systems, home-appliance controllers, and weapon systems are also real-time systems.

A real-time system has well-defined, fixed time constraints. Processing *must* be done within the defined constraints, or the system will fail. For instance, it would not do for a robot arm to be instructed to halt *after* it had smashed into the car it was building. A real-time system functions correctly only if it returns the correct result within its time constraints. Contrast this system with a time-sharing system, where it is desirable (but not mandatory) to respond quickly, or a batch system, which may have no time constraints at all.

In Chapter 19, we cover real-time embedded systems in great detail. In Chapter 5, we consider the scheduling facility needed to implement real-time functionality in an operating system. In Chapter 9, we describe the design of memory management for real-time computing. Finally, in Chapter 22, we describe the real-time components of the Windows XP operating system.

1.11.2 Multimedia Systems

Most operating systems are designed to handle conventional data such as text files, programs, word-processing documents, and spreadsheets. However, a recent trend in technology is the incorporation of **multimedia data** into computer systems. Multimedia data consist of audio and video files as well as conventional files. These data differ from conventional data in that multimedia data—such as frames of video—must be delivered (streamed) according to certain time restrictions (for example, 30 frames per second).

Multimedia describes a wide range of applications in popular use today. These include audio files such as MP3, DVD movies, video conferencing, and short video clips of movie previews or news stories downloaded over the Internet. Multimedia applications may also include live webcasts (broadcasting over the World Wide Web) of speeches or sporting events and even live webcams that allow a viewer in Manhattan to observe customers at a cafe in Paris. Multimedia applications need not be either audio or video; rather, a multimedia application often includes a combination of both. For example, a movie may consist of separate audio and video tracks. Nor must multimedia applications be delivered only to desktop personal computers. Increasingly, they are being directed toward smaller devices, including PDAs and cellular telephones. For example, a stock trader may have stock quotes delivered wirelessly and in real time to his PDA.

In Chapter 20, we explore the demands of multimedia applications, describe how multimedia data differ from conventional data, and explain how the nature of these data affects the design of operating systems that support the requirements of multimedia systems.

1.11.3 Handheld Systems

Handheld systems include personal digital assistants (PDAs), such as Palm and Pocket-PCs, and cellular telephones, many of which use special-purpose embedded operating systems. Developers of handheld systems and applications face many challenges, most of which are due to the limited size of such devices. For example, a PDA is typically about 5 inches in height and 3 inches in width, and it weighs less than one-half pound. Because of their size, most handheld devices have small amounts of memory, slow processors, and small display screens. We take a look now at each of these limitations.

The amount of physical memory in a handheld depends on the device, but typically it is somewhere between 1 MB and 1 GB. (Contrast this with a typical PC or workstation, which may have several gigabytes of memory.) As a result, the operating system and applications must manage memory efficiently. This includes returning all allocated memory to the memory manager when the memory is not being used. In Chapter 9, we explore virtual memory, which allows developers to write programs that behave as if the system has more memory than is physically available. Currently, not many handheld devices use virtual memory techniques, so program developers must work within the confines of limited physical memory.

A second issue of concern to developers of handheld devices is the speed of the processor used in the devices. Processors for most handheld devices run at a fraction of the speed of a processor in a PC. Faster processors require more power. To include a faster processor in a handheld device would require a larger battery, which would take up more space and would have to be replaced (or recharged) more frequently. Most handheld devices use smaller, slower processors that consume less power. Therefore, the operating system and applications must be designed not to tax the processor.

The last issue confronting program designers for handheld devices is I/O. A lack of physical space limits input methods to small keyboards, handwriting recognition, or small screen-based keyboards. The small display screens limit output options. Whereas a monitor for a home computer may measure up to 30 inches, the display for a handheld device is often no more than 3 inches square. Familiar tasks, such as reading e-mail and browsing Web pages, must be condensed into smaller displays. One approach for displaying the content in Web pages is **Web clipping**, where only a small subset of a Web page is delivered and displayed on the handheld device.

Some handheld devices use wireless technology, such as BlueTooth or 802.11, allowing remote access to e-mail and Web browsing. Cellular telephones with connectivity to the Internet fall into this category. However, for PDAs that do not provide wireless access, downloading data typically requires the user first to download the data to a PC or workstation and then download the data to the PDA. Some PDAs allow data to be directly copied from one device to another using an infrared link.

Generally, the limitations in the functionality of PDAs are balanced by their convenience and portability. Their use continues to expand as network connections become more available and other options, such as digital cameras and MP3 players, expand their utility.

1.12   Computing Environments

So far, we have provided an overview of computer-system organization and major operating-system components. We conclude with a brief overview of how these are used in a variety of computing environments.

1.12.1 Traditional Computing

As computing matures, the lines separating many of the traditional computing environments are blurring. Consider the "typical office environment." Just a few years ago, this environment consisted of PCs connected to a network, with servers providing file and print services. Remote access was awkward, and portability was achieved by use of laptop computers. Terminals attached to mainframes were prevalent at many companies as well, with even fewer remote access and portability options.

The current trend is toward providing more ways to access these computing environments. Web technologies are stretching the boundaries of traditional computing. Companies establish **portals**, which provide Web accessibility to their internal servers. **Network computers** are essentially terminals that understand Web-based computing. Handheld computers can synchronize with

PCs to allow very portable use of company information. Handheld PDAs can also connect to **wireless networks** to use the company's Web portal (as well as the myriad other Web resources).

At home, most users had a single computer with a slow modem connection to the office, the Internet, or both. Today, network-connection speeds once available only at great cost are relatively inexpensive, giving home users more access to more data. These fast data connections are allowing home computers to serve up Web pages and to run networks that include printers, client PCs, and servers. Some homes even have **firewalls** to protect their networks from security breaches. Those firewalls cost thousands of dollars a few years ago and did not even exist a decade ago.

In the latter half of the previous century, computing resources were scarce. (Before that, they were nonexistent!) For a period of time, systems were either batch or interactive. Batch systems processed jobs in bulk, with predetermined input (from files or other sources of data). Interactive systems waited for input from users. To optimize the use of the computing resources, multiple users shared time on these systems. Time-sharing systems used a timer and scheduling algorithms to rapidly cycle processes through the CPU, giving each user a share of the resources.

Today, traditional time-sharing systems are uncommon. The same scheduling technique is still in use on workstations and servers, but frequently the processes are all owned by the same user (or a single user and the operating system). User processes, and system processes that provide services to the user, are managed so that each frequently gets a slice of computer time. Consider the windows created while a user is working on a PC, for example, and the fact that they may be performing different tasks at the same time.

1.12.2   Client–Server Computing

As PCs have become faster, more powerful, and cheaper, designers have shifted away from centralized system architecture. Terminals connected to centralized systems are now being supplanted by PCs. Correspondingly, user-interface functionality once handled directly by centralized systems is increasingly being handled by PCs. As a result, many of today's systems act as **server systems** to satisfy requests generated by **client systems**. This form of specialized distributed system, called a **client–server** system, has the general structure depicted in Figure 1.13.

Server systems can be broadly categorized as compute servers and file servers:

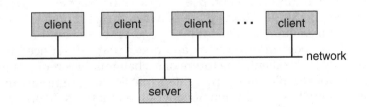

Figure 1.13   General structure of a client–server system.

- The **compute-server system** provides an interface to which a client can send a request to perform an action (for example, read data); in response, the server executes the action and sends back results to the client. A server running a database that responds to client requests for data is an example of such a system.

- The **file-server system** provides a file-system interface where clients can create, update, read, and delete files. An example of such a system is a Web server that delivers files to clients running Web browsers.

1.12.3 Peer-to-Peer Computing

Another structure for a distributed system is the peer-to-peer (P2P) system model. In this model, clients and servers are not distinguished from one another; instead, all nodes within the system are considered peers, and each may act as either a client or a server, depending on whether it is requesting or providing a service. Peer-to-peer systems offer an advantage over traditional client-server systems. In a client-server system, the server is a bottleneck; but in a peer-to-peer system, services can be provided by several nodes distributed throughout the network.

To participate in a peer-to-peer system, a node must first join the network of peers. Once a node has joined the network, it can begin providing services to—and requesting services from—other nodes in the network. Determining what services are available is accomplished in one of two general ways:

- When a node joins a network, it registers its service with a centralized lookup service on the network. Any node desiring a specific service first contacts this centralized lookup service to determine which node provides the service. The remainder of the communication takes place between the client and the service provider.

- A peer acting as a client must first discover what node provides a desired service by broadcasting a request for the service to all other nodes in the network. The node (or nodes) providing that service responds to the peer making the request. To support this approach, a *discovery protocol* must be provided that allows peers to discover services provided by other peers in the network.

Peer-to-peer networks gained widespread popularity in the late 1990s with several file-sharing services, such as Napster and Gnutella, that enable peers to exchange files with one another. The Napster system uses an approach similar to the first type described above: a centralized server maintains an index of all files stored on peer nodes in the Napster network, and the actual exchanging of files takes place between the peer nodes. The Gnutella system uses a technique similar to the second type: a client broadcasts file requests to other nodes in the system, and nodes that can service the request respond directly to the client. The future of exchanging files remains uncertain because many of the files are copyrighted (music, for example), and there are laws governing the distribution of copyrighted material. In any case, though, peer-to-peer technology undoubtedly will play a role in the future of many services, such as searching, file exchange, and e-mail.

1.12.4 Web-Based Computing

The Web has become ubiquitous, leading to more access by a wider variety of devices than was dreamt of a few years ago. PCs are still the most prevalent access devices, with workstations, handheld PDAs, and even cell phones also providing access.

Web computing has increased the emphasis on networking. Devices that were not previously networked now include wired or wireless access. Devices that were networked now have faster network connectivity, provided by either improved networking technology, optimized network implementation code, or both.

The implementation of Web-based computing has given rise to new categories of devices, such as load balancers, which distribute network connections among a pool of similar servers. Operating systems like Windows 95, which acted as Web clients, have evolved into Linux and Windows XP, which can act as Web servers as well as clients. Generally, the Web has increased the complexity of devices because their users require them to be Web-enabled.

1.13 Open-Source Operating Systems

The study of operating systems, as noted earlier, is made easier by the availability of a vast number of open-source releases. Open-source operating systems are those made available in source-code format rather than as compiled binary code. Linux is the most famous open-source operating system, while Microsoft Windows is a well-known example of the opposite closed-source approach. Starting with the source code allows the programmer to produce binary code that can be executed on a system. Doing the opposite—reverse engineering the source code from the binaries—is quite a lot of work, and useful items such as comments are never recovered. Learning operating systems by examining the actual source code, rather than reading summaries of that code, can be extremely useful. With the source code in hand, a student can modify the operating system and then compile and run the code to try out those changes, which is another excellent learning tool. This text includes projects that involve modifying operating system source code, while also describing algorithms at a high level to be sure all important operating system topics are covered. Throughout the text, we provide pointers to examples of open-source code for deeper study.

There are many benefits to open-source operating systems, including a community of interested (and usually unpaid) programmers who contribute to the code by helping to debug it, analyze it, provide support, and suggest changes. Arguably, open-source code is more secure than closed-source code because many more eyes are viewing the code. Certainly open-source code has bugs, but open-source advocates argue that bugs tend to be found and fixed faster owing to the number of people using and viewing the code. Companies that earn revenue from selling their programs tend to be hesitant to open-source their code, but Red Hat, SUSE, Sun, and a myriad of other companies are doing just that and showing that commercial companies benefit, rather than suffer, when they open-source their code. Revenue can be generated through support contracts and the sale of hardware on which the software runs, for example.

1.13.1 History

In the early days of modern computing (that is, the 1950s), a great deal of software was available in open-source format. The original hackers (computer enthusiasts) at MIT's Tech Model Railroad Club left their programs in drawers for others to work on. "Homebrew" user groups exchanged code during their meetings. Later, company-specific user groups, such as Digital Equipment Corporation's DEC, accepted contributions of source-code programs, collected them onto tapes, and distributed the tapes to interested members.

Computer and software companies eventually sought to limit the use of their software to authorized computers and paying customers. Releasing only the binary files compiled from the source code, rather than the source code itself, helped them to achieve this goal, as well as protecting their code and their ideas from their competitors. Another issue involved copyrighted material. Operating systems and other programs can limit the ability to play back movies and music or display electronic books to authorized computers. Such **copy protection** or **Digital Rights Management (DRM)** would not be effective if the source code that implemented these limits were published. Laws in many countries, including the U.S. Digital Millennium Copyright Act (DMCA), make it illegal to reverse-engineer DRM code or otherwise try to circumvent copy protection.

To counter the move to limit software use and redistribution, Richard Stallman in 1983 started the GNU project to create a free, open-source UNIX-compatible operating system. In 1985, he published the GNU Manifesto, which argues that all software should be free and open-sourced. He also formed the **Free Software Foundation (FSF)** with the goal of encouraging the free exchange of software source code and the free use of that software. Rather than copyright its software, the FSF "copylefts" the software to encourage sharing and improvement. The **GNU General Public License (GPL)** codifies copylefting and is a common license under which free software is released. Fundamentally, GPL requires that the source code be distributed with any binaries and that any changes made to the source code be released under the same GPL license.

1.13.2 Linux

As an example of an open-source operating system, consider GNU/Linux. The GNU project produced many UNIX-compatible tools, including compilers, editors, and utilities, but never released a kernel. In 1991, a student in Finland, Linus Torvalds, released a rudimentary UNIX-like kernel using the GNU compilers and tools and invited contributions worldwide. The advent of the Internet meant that anyone interested could download the source code, modify it, and submit changes to Torvalds. Releasing updates once a week allowed this so-called Linux operating system to grow rapidly, enhanced by several thousand programmers.

The resulting GNU/Linux operating system has spawned hundreds of unique **distributions**, or custom builds, of the system. Major distributions include RedHat, SUSE, Fedora, Debian, Slackware, and Ubuntu. Distributions vary in function, utility, installed applications, hardware support, user interface, and purpose. For example, RedHat Enterprise Linux is geared to large commercial use. PCLinuxOS is a **LiveCD**—an operating system that can be booted and run from a CD-ROM without being installed on a system's hard disk. One variant of PCLinuxOS, "PCLinuxOS Supergamer DVD," is a **LiveDVD** that includes graphics drivers and games. A gamer can run it on any compatible system simply by booting from the DVD. When the gamer is finished, a reboot of the system resets it to its installed operating system.

Access to the Linux source code varies by release. Here, we consider Ubuntu Linux. Ubuntu is a popular Linux distribution that comes in a variety of types, including those tuned for desktops, servers, and students. Its founder pays for the printing and mailing of DVDs containing the binary and source code (which helps to make it popular). The following steps outline a way to explore the Ubuntu kernel source code on systems that support the free "VMware Player" tool:

- Download the player from `http://www.vmware.com/download/player/` and install it on your system.

- Download a virtual machine containing Ubuntu. Hundreds of "appliances", or virtual machine images, pre-installed with operating systems and applications, are available from VMware at `http://www.vmware.com/appliances/`.

- Boot the virtual machine within VMware Player.

- Get the source code of the kernel release of interest, such as 2.6, by executing `wget http://www.kernel.org/pub/linux/kernel/v2.6/linux-2.6.18.1.tar.bz2` within the Ubuntu virtual machine.

- Uncompress and untar the downloaded file via `tar xjf linux-2.6.18.1.tar.bz2`.

- Explore the source code of the Ubuntu kernel, which is now in `./linux-2.6.18.1`.

For more about Linux, see Chapter 21. For more about virtual machines, see Section 2.8.

1.13.3 BSD UNIX

BSD UNIX has a longer and more complicated history than Linux. It started in 1978 as a derivative of AT&T's UNIX. Releases from the University of California at Berkeley (UCB) came in source and binary form, but they were not open-source because a license from AT&T was required. BSD UNIX's development was slowed by a lawsuit by AT&T, but eventually a fully functional, open-source version, 4.4BSD-lite, was released in 1994.

Just as with Linux, there are many distributions of BSD UNIX, including FreeBSD, NetBSD, OpenBSD, and DragonflyBSD. To explore the source code of FreeBSD, simply download the virtual machine image of the version of interest and boot it within VMware, as described above for Ubuntu Linux. The source code comes with the distribution and is stored in `/usr/src/`. The kernel source code is in `/usr/src/sys`. For example, to examine the virtual-memory implementation code in the FreeBSD kernel, see the files in `/usr/src/sys/vm`.

Darwin, the core kernel component of MAC, is based on BSD UNIX and is open-sourced as well. That source code is available from `http://www.opensource.apple.com/darwinsource/`. Every MAC release has its open-source components posted at that site. The name of the package that contains the kernel is "xnu." The source code for MAC kernel revision 1228 (the source code to MAC Leopard) can be found at www.opensource.apple.com/darwinsource/tarballs/apsl/xnu-1228.tar.gz. Apple also provides extensive developer tools, documentation, and support at http://connect.apple.com. For more information, see Appendix A.

1.13.4 Solaris

Solaris is the commercial UNIX-based operating system of Sun Microsystems. Originally, Sun's SunOS operating system was based on BSD UNIX. Sun moved to AT&T's System V UNIX as its base in 1991. In 2005, Sun open-sourced some of the Solaris code, and over time, the company has added more and more to that open-source code base. Unfortunately, not all of Solaris is open-sourced, because some of the code is still owned by AT&T and other companies. However, Solaris can be compiled from the open source and linked with binaries of the close-sourced components, so it can still be explored, modified, compiled, and tested.

The source code is available from http://opensolaris.org/os/downloads/. Also available there are pre-compiled distributions based on the source code, documentation, and discussion groups. It is not necessary to download the entire source-code bundle from the site, because Sun allows visitors to explore the source code on-line via a source code browser.

1.13.5 Utility

The free software movement is driving legions of programmers to create thousands of open-source projects, including operating systems. Sites like http://freshmeat.net/ and http://distrowatch.com/ provide portals to many of these projects. Open-source projects enable students to use source code as a learning tool. They can modify programs and test them, help find and fix bugs, and otherwise explore mature, full-featured operating systems, compilers, tools, user interfaces, and other types of programs. The availability of source code for historic projects, such as Multics, can help students to understand those projects and to build knowledge that will help in the implementation of new projects.

GNU/Linux, BSD UNIX, and Solaris are all open-source operating systems, but each has its own goals, utility, licensing, and purpose. Sometimes licenses are not mutually exclusive and cross-pollination occurs, allowing rapid improvements in operating-system projects. For example, several major components of Solaris have been ported to BSD UNIX. The advantages of free software and open sourcing are likely to increase the number and quality of open-source projects, leading to an increase in the number of individuals and companies that use these projects.

1.14 Summary

An operating system is software that manages the computer hardware, as well as providing an environment for application programs to run. Perhaps the most visible aspect of an operating system is the interface to the computer system it provides to the human user.

For a computer to do its job of executing programs, the programs must be in main memory. Main memory is the only large storage area that the processor can access directly. It is an array of words or bytes, ranging in size from millions to billions. Each word in memory has its own address. The main memory is usually a volatile storage device that loses its contents when power is turned off or lost. Most computer systems provide secondary storage as an extension of main memory. Secondary storage provides a form of nonvolatile storage that is capable of holding large quantities of data permanently. The most common secondary-storage device is a magnetic disk, which provides storage of both programs and data.

The wide variety of storage systems in a computer system can be organized in a hierarchy according to speed and cost. The higher levels are expensive, but they are fast. As we move down the hierarchy, the cost per bit generally decreases, whereas the access time generally increases.

There are several different strategies for designing a computer system. Uniprocessor systems have only a single processor, while multiprocessor systems contain two or more processors that share physical memory and peripheral devices. The most common multiprocessor design is symmetric multiprocessing (or SMP), where all processors are considered peers and run independently of one another. Clustered systems are a specialized form of multiprocessor systems and consist of multiple computer systems connected by a local area network.

To best utilize the CPU, modern operating systems employ multiprogramming, which allows several jobs to be in memory at the same time, thus ensuring that the CPU always has a job to execute. Time-sharing systems are an extension of multiprogramming wherein CPU scheduling algorithms rapidly switch between jobs, thus providing the illusion that each job is running concurrently.

The operating system must ensure correct operation of the computer system. To prevent user programs from interfering with the proper operation of the system, the hardware has two modes: user mode and kernel mode. Various instructions (such as I/O instructions and halt instructions) are privileged and can be executed only in kernel mode. The memory in which the operating system resides must also be protected from modification by the user. A timer prevents infinite loops. These facilities (dual mode, privileged instructions, memory protection, and timer interrupt) are basic building blocks used by operating systems to achieve correct operation.

A process (or job) is the fundamental unit of work in an operating system. Process management includes creating and deleting processes and providing mechanisms for processes to communicate and synchronize with each other. An operating system manages memory by keeping track of what parts of memory are being used and by whom. The operating system is also responsible for dynamically allocating and freeing memory space. Storage space is also managed by the operating system; this includes providing file systems for representing files and directories and managing space on mass-storage devices.

Operating systems must also be concerned with protecting and securing the operating system and users. Protection measures are mechanisms that control the access of processes or users to the resources made available by the computer system. Security measures are responsible for defending a computer system from external or internal attacks.

Distributed systems allow users to share resources on geographically dispersed hosts connected via a computer network. Services may be provided through either the client–server model or the peer-to-peer model. In a clustered system, multiple machines can perform computations on data residing on shared storage, and computing can continue even when some subset of cluster members fails.

LANs and WANs are the two basic types of networks. LANs enable processors distributed over a small geographical area to communicate, whereas WANs allow processors distributed over a larger area to communicate. LANs typically are faster than WANs.

There are several computer systems that serve specific purposes. These include real-time operating systems designed for embedded environments such as consumer devices, automobiles, and robotics. Real-time operating systems have well-defined, fixed-time constraints. Processing *must* be done within the defined constraints, or the system will fail. Multimedia systems involve the delivery of multimedia data and often have special requirements of displaying or playing audio, video, or synchronized audio and video streams.

Recently, the influence of the Internet and the World Wide Web has encouraged the development of operating systems that include Web browsers and networking and communication software as integral features.

The free software movement has created thousands of open-source projects, including operating systems. Because of these projects, students are able to use source code as a learning tool. They can modify programs and test them, help find and fix bugs, and otherwise explore mature, full-featured operating systems, compilers, tools, user interfaces, and other types of programs.

GNU/Linux, BSD UNIX, and Solaris are all open-source operating systems. The advantages of free software and open sourcing are likely to increase the number and quality of open-source projects, leading to an increase in the number of individuals and companies that use these projects.

Practice Exercises

1.1   What are the three main purposes of an operating system?

1.2   What are the main differences between operating systems for mainframe computers and personal computers?

1.3   List the four steps that are necessary to run a program on a completely dedicated machine—a computer that is running only that program.

1.4   We have stressed the need for an operating system to make efficient use of the computing hardware. When is it appropriate for the operating system to forsake this principle and to "waste" resources? Why is such a system not really wasteful?

1.5   What is the main difficulty that a programmer must overcome in writing an operating system for a real-time environment?

1.6   Consider the various definitions of *operating system*. Consider whether the operating system should include applications such as Web browsers and mail programs. Argue both that it should and that it should not, and support your answers.

1.7 How does the distinction between kernel mode and user mode function as a rudimentary form of protection (security) system?

1.8 Which of the following instructions should be privileged?

a. Set value of timer.

b. Read the clock.

c. Clear memory.

d. Issue a trap instruction.

e. Turn off interrupts.

f. Modify entries in device-status table.

g. Switch from user to kernel mode.

h. Access I/O device.

1.9 Some early computers protected the operating system by placing it in a memory partition that could not be modified by either the user job or the operating system itself. Describe two difficulties that you think could arise with such a scheme.

1.10 Some CPUs provide for more than two modes of operation. What are two possible uses of these multiple modes?

1.11 Timers could be used to compute the current time. Provide a short description of how this could be accomplished.

1.12 Is the Internet a LAN or a WAN?

Exercises

1.13 In a multiprogramming and time-sharing environment, several users share the system simultaneously. This situation can result in various security problems.

a. What are two such problems?

b. Can we ensure the same degree of security in a time-shared machine as in a dedicated machine? Explain your answer.

1.14 The issue of resource utilization shows up in different forms in different types of operating systems. List what resources must be managed carefully in the following settings:

a. Mainframe or minicomputer systems

b. Workstations connected to servers

c. Handheld computers

1.15   Under what circumstances would a user be better off using a time-sharing system rather than a PC or a single-user workstation?

1.16   Identify which of the functionalities listed below need to be supported by the operating system for (a) handheld devices and (b) real-time systems.

    a.   Batch programming

    b.   Virtual memory

    c.   Time sharing

1.17   Describe the differences between symmetric and asymmetric multiprocessing. What are three advantages and one disadvantage of multiprocessor systems?

1.18   How do clustered systems differ from multiprocessor systems? What is required for two machines belonging to a cluster to cooperate to provide a highly available service?

1.19   Distinguish between the client–server and peer-to-peer models of distributed systems.

1.20   Consider a computing cluster consisting of two nodes running a database. Describe two ways in which the cluster software can manage access to the data on the disk. Discuss the benefits and disadvantages of each.

1.21   How are network computers different from traditional personal computers? Describe some usage scenarios in which it is advantageous to use network computers.

1.22   What is the purpose of interrupts? What are the differences between a trap and an interrupt? Can traps be generated intentionally by a user program? If so, for what purpose?

1.23   Direct memory access is used for high-speed I/O devices in order to avoid increasing the CPU's execution load.

    a.   How does the CPU interface with the device to coordinate the transfer?

    b.   How does the CPU know when the memory operations are complete?

    c.   The CPU is allowed to execute other programs while the DMA controller is transferring data. Does this process interfere with the execution of the user programs? If so, describe what forms of interference are caused.

1.24   Some computer systems do not provide a privileged mode of operation in hardware. Is it possible to construct a secure operating system for these computer systems? Give arguments both that it is and that it is not possible.

1.25   Give two reasons why caches are useful. What problems do they solve? What problems do they cause? If a cache can be made as large as the device for which it is caching (for instance, a cache as large as a disk), why not make it that large and eliminate the device?

1.26 Consider an SMP system similar to what is shown in Figure 1.6. Illustrate with an example how data residing in memory could in fact have two different values in each of the local caches.

1.27 Discuss, with examples, how the problem of maintaining coherence of cached data manifests itself in the following processing environments:

    a. Single-processor systems

    b. Multiprocessor systems

    c. Distributed systems

1.28 Describe a mechanism for enforcing memory protection in order to prevent a program from modifying the memory associated with other programs.

1.29 What network configuration would best suit the following environments?

    a. A dormitory floor

    b. A university campus

    c. A state

    d. A nation

1.30 Define the essential properties of the following types of operating systems:

    a. Batch

    b. Interactive

    c. Time sharing

    d. Real time

    e. Network

    f. Parallel

    g. Distributed

    h. Clustered

    i. Handheld

1.31 What are the tradeoffs inherent in handheld computers?

1.32 Identify several advantages and several disadvantages of open-source operating systems. Include the types of people who would find each aspect to be an advantage or a disadvantage.

Wiley Plus

Visit Wiley Plus for

- Source code

- Solutions to practice exercises

- Additional programming problems and exercises

- Labs using an operating system simulator

Bibliographical Notes

Brookshear [2003] provides an overview of computer science in general.

An overview of the Linux operating system is presented in Bovet and Cesati [2006]. Solomon and Russinovich [2000] give an overview of Microsoft Windows and considerable technical detail about the system internals and components. Russinovich and Solomon [2005] update this information to Windows Server 2003 and Windows XP. McDougall and Mauro [2007] cover the internals of the Solaris operating system. Mac OS X is presented at http://www.apple.com/macosx. Mac OS X internals are discussed in Singh [2007].

Coverage of peer-to-peer systems includes Parameswaran et al. [2001], Gong [2002], Ripeanu et al. [2002], Agre [2003], Balakrishnan et al. [2003], and Loo [2003]. A discussion of peer-to-peer file-sharing systems can be found in Lee [2003]. Good coverage of cluster computing is provided by Buyya [1999]. Recent advances in cluster computing are described by Ahmed [2000]. A survey of issues relating to operating-system support for distributed systems can be found in Tanenbaum and Van Renesse [1985].

Many general textbooks cover operating systems, including Stallings [2000b], Nutt [2004], and Tanenbaum [2001].

Hamacher et al. [2002] describe computer organization, and McDougall and Laudon [2006] discuss multicore processors. Hennessy and Patterson [2007] provide coverage of I/O systems and buses, and of system architecture in general. Blaauw and Brooks [1997] describe details of the architecture of many computer systems, including several from IBM. Stokes [2007] provides an illustrated introduction to microprocessors and computer architecture.

Cache memories, including associative memory, are described and analyzed by Smith [1982]. That paper also includes an extensive bibliography on the subject.

Discussions concerning magnetic-disk technology are presented by Freedman [1983] and by Harker et al. [1981]. Optical disks are covered by Kenville [1982], Fujitani [1984], O'Leary and Kitts [1985], Gait [1988], and Olsen and Kenley [1989]. Discussions of floppy disks are offered by Pechura and Schoeffler [1983] and by Sarisky [1983]. General discussions concerning mass-storage technology are offered by Chi [1982] and by Hoagland [1985].

Kurose and Ross [2005] and Tanenbaum [2003] provides general overviews of computer networks. Fortier [1989] presents a detailed discussion of networking hardware and software. Kozierok [2005] discuss TCP in detail. Mullender [1993] provides an overview of distributed systems. Wolf [2003] discusses recent developments in developing embedded systems. Issues related to hand-held devices can be found in Myers and Beigl [2003] and Di Pietro and Mancini [2003].

A full discussion of the history of open sourcing and its benefits and challenges is found in Raymond [1999]. The history of hacking is discussed in Levy [1994]. The Free Software Foundation has published its philosophy on its Web site: `http://www.gnu.org/philosophy/free-software-for-freedom.html`. Detailed instructions on how to build the Ubuntu Linux kernel are on `http://www.howtoforge.com/kernel_compilation_ubuntu`. The open-source components of MAC are available from `http://developer.apple.com/open-source/index.html`.

Wikipedia (`http://en.wikipedia.org/wiki/Richard_Stallman`) has an informative entry about Richard Stallman.

The source code of Multics is available at `http://web.mit.edu/multics-history/source/Multics_Internet_Server/Multics_sources.html`.

Operating-System Structures

An operating system provides the environment within which programs are executed. Internally, operating systems vary greatly in their makeup, since they are organized along many different lines. The design of a new operating system is a major task. It is important that the goals of the system be well defined before the design begins. These goals form the basis for choices among various algorithms and strategies.

We can view an operating system from several vantage points. One view focuses on the services that the system provides; another, on the interface that it makes available to users and programmers; a third, on its components and their interconnections. In this chapter, we explore all three aspects of operating systems, showing the viewpoints of users, programmers, and operating-system designers. We consider what services an operating system provides, how they are provided, how they are debugged, and what the various methodologies are for designing such systems. Finally, we describe how operating systems are created and how a computer starts its operating system.

CHAPTER OBJECTIVES

- To describe the services an operating system provides to users, processes, and other systems.
- To discuss the various ways of structuring an operating system.
- To explain how operating systems are installed and customized and how they boot.

2.1 Operating-System Services

An operating system provides an environment for the execution of programs. It provides certain services to programs and to the users of those programs. The specific services provided, of course, differ from one operating system to another, but we can identify common classes. These operating-system services are provided for the convenience of the programmer, to make the programming

49

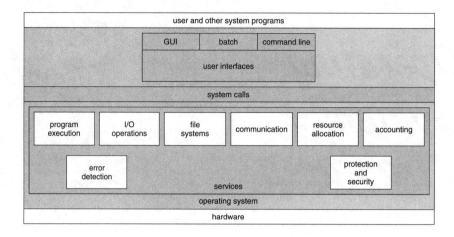

Figure 2.1   A view of operating system services.

task easier. Figure 2.1 shows one view of the various operating-system services and how they interrelate.

One set of operating-system services provides functions that are helpful to the user.

- **User interface**. Almost all operating systems have a **user interface** (UI). This interface can take several forms. One is a **DTrace command-line interface (CLI)**, which uses text commands and a method for entering them (say, a program to allow entering and editing of commands). Another is a **batch interface**, in which commands and directives to control those commands are entered into files, and those files are executed. Most commonly, a **graphical user interface (GUI)** is used. Here, the interface is a window system with a pointing device to direct I/O, choose from menus, and make selections and a keyboard to enter text. Some systems provide two or all three of these variations.

- **Program execution**. The system must be able to load a program into memory and to run that program. The program must be able to end its execution, either normally or abnormally (indicating error).

- **I/O operations**. A running program may require I/O, which may involve a file or an I/O device. For specific devices, special functions may be desired (such as recording to a CD or DVD drive or blanking a display screen). For efficiency and protection, users usually cannot control I/O devices directly. Therefore, the operating system must provide a means to do I/O.

- **File-system manipulation**. The file system is of particular interest. Obviously, programs need to read and write files and directories. They also need to create and delete them by name, search for a given file, and list file information. Finally, some programs include permissions management to allow or deny access to files or directories based on file ownership. Many operating systems provide a variety of file systems, sometimes to allow personal choice, and sometimes to provide specific features or performance characteristics.

- **Communications**. There are many circumstances in which one process needs to exchange information with another process. Such communication may occur between processes that are executing on the same computer or between processes that are executing on different computer systems tied together by a computer network. Communications may be implemented via *shared memory* or through *message passing*, in which packets of information are moved between processes by the operating system.

- **Error detection**. The operating system needs to be constantly aware of possible errors. Errors may occur in the CPU and memory hardware (such as a memory error or a power failure), in I/O devices (such as a parity error on tape, a connection failure on a network, or lack of paper in the printer), and in the user program (such as an arithmetic overflow, an attempt to access an illegal memory location, or a too-great use of CPU time). For each type of error, the operating system should take the appropriate action to ensure correct and consistent computing. Of course, there is variation in how operating systems react to and correct errors. Debugging facilities can greatly enhance the user's and programmer's abilities to use the system efficiently.

Another set of operating-system functions exists not for helping the user but rather for ensuring the efficient operation of the system itself. Systems with multiple users can gain efficiency by sharing the computer resources among the users.

- **Resource allocation**. When there are multiple users or multiple jobs running at the same time, resources must be allocated to each of them. Many different types of resources are managed by the operating system. Some (such as CPU cycles, main memory, and file storage) may have special allocation code, whereas others (such as I/O devices) may have much more general request and release code. For instance, in determining how best to use the CPU, operating systems have CPU-scheduling routines that take into account the speed of the CPU, the jobs that must be executed, the number of registers available, and other factors. There may also be routines to allocate printers, modems, USB storage drives, and other peripheral devices.

- **Accounting**. We want to keep track of which users use how much and what kinds of computer resources. This record keeping may be used for accounting (so that users can be billed) or simply for accumulating usage statistics. Usage statistics may be a valuable tool for researchers who wish to reconfigure the system to improve computing services.

- **Protection and security**. The owners of information stored in a multiuser or networked computer system may want to control use of that information. When several separate processes execute concurrently, it should not be possible for one process to interfere with the others or with the operating system itself. Protection involves ensuring that all access to system resources is controlled. Security of the system from outsiders is also important. Such security starts with requiring each user to authenticate himself or herself to the system, usually by means of a password, to gain access to system resources. It extends to defending external I/O devices, including modems and network adapters, from invalid access attempts and to recording all such connections for detection of break-ins. If a system is to be protected and secure, precautions must be instituted throughout it. A chain is only as strong as its weakest link.

2.2 User Operating-System Interface

We mentioned earlier that there are several ways for users to interface with the operating system. Here, we discuss two fundamental approaches. One provides a command-line interface, or **command interpreter**, that allows users to directly enter commands to be performed by the operating system. The other allows users to interface with the operating system via a graphical user interface, or GUI.

2.2.1 Command Interpreter

Some operating systems include the command interpreter in the kernel. Others, such as Windows XP and UNIX, treat the command interpreter as a special program that is running when a job is initiated or when a user first logs on (on interactive systems). On systems with multiple command interpreters to choose from, the interpreters are known as **shells**. For example, on UNIX and Linux systems, a user may choose among several different shells, including the *Bourne shell, C shell, Bourne-Again shell, Korn shell,* and others. Third-party shells and free user-written shells are also available. Most shells provide similar functionality, and a user's choice of which shell to use is generally based on personal preference. Figure 2.2 shows the Bourne shell command interpreter being used on Solaris 10.

The main function of the command interpreter is to get and execute the next user-specified command. Many of the commands given at this level manipulate files: create, delete, list, print, copy, execute, and so on. The MS-DOS and UNIX shells operate in this way. These commands can be implemented in two general ways.

In one approach, the command interpreter itself contains the code to execute the command. For example, a command to delete a file may cause the command interpreter to jump to a section of its code that sets up the parameters and makes the appropriate system call. In this case, the number of commands that can be given determines the size of the command interpreter, since each command requires its own implementing code.

An alternative approach—used by UNIX, among other operating systems —implements most commands through system programs. In this case, the command interpreter does not understand the command in any way; it merely uses the command to identify a file to be loaded into memory and executed. Thus, the UNIX command to delete a file

```
rm file.txt
```

would search for a file called `rm`, load the file into memory, and execute it with the parameter `file.txt`. The function associated with the `rm` command would be defined completely by the code in the file `rm`. In this way, programmers can add new commands to the system easily by creating new files with the proper

```
🔽                          🖳 Terminal                        ⊟ ⊡ ⊠

 File  Edit  View  Terminal  Tabs  Help
fd0         0.0    0.0    0.0     0.0  0.0  0.0    0.0    0   0      ▲
sd0         0.0    0.2    0.0     0.2  0.0  0.0    0.4    0   0
sd1         0.0    0.0    0.0     0.0  0.0  0.0    0.0    0   0
                      extended device statistics
device      r/s    w/s    kr/s    kw/s wait actv  svc_t  %w  %b
fd0         0.0    0.0    0.0     0.0  0.0  0.0    0.0    0   0
sd0         0.6    0.0    38.4    0.0  0.0  0.0    8.2    0   0
sd1         0.0    0.0    0.0     0.0  0.0  0.0    0.0    0   0
(root@pbg-nv64-vm)-(11/pts)-(00:53 15-Jun-2007)-(global)
-(/var/tmp/system-contents/scripts)# swap -sh
total: 1.1G allocated + 190M reserved = 1.3G used, 1.6G available
(root@pbg-nv64-vm)-(12/pts)-(00:53 15-Jun-2007)-(global)
-(/var/tmp/system-contents/scripts)# uptime
 12:53am  up 9 min(s),  3 users,  load average: 33.29, 67.68, 36.81
(root@pbg-nv64-vm)-(13/pts)-(00:53 15-Jun-2007)-(global)
-(/var/tmp/system-contents/scripts)# w
  4:07pm  up 17 day(s), 15:24,  3 users,  load average: 0.09, 0.11, 8.66
User        tty            login@  idle   JCPU   PCPU  what
root        console        15Jun0718days     1           /usr/bin/ssh-agent -- /usr/bi
n/d
root        pts/3          15Jun07          18     4  w
root        pts/4          15Jun0718days               w
(root@pbg-nv64-vm)-(14/pts)-(16:07 02-Jul-2007)-(global)
-(/var/tmp/system-contents/scripts)#                               ▼
```

Figure 2.2   The Bourne shell command interpreter in Solaris 10.

names. The command-interpreter program, which can be small, does not have to be changed for new commands to be added.

2.2.2   Graphical User Interfaces

A second strategy for interfacing with the operating system is through a user-friendly graphical user interface, or GUI. Here, rather than entering commands directly via a command-line interface, users employ a mouse-based window-and-menu system characterized by a **desktop** metaphor. The user moves the mouse to position its pointer on images, or **icons**, on the screen (the desktop) that represent programs, files, directories, and system functions. Depending on the mouse pointer's location, clicking a button on the mouse can invoke a program, select a file or directory—known as a **folder**—or pull down a menu that contains commands.

Graphical user interfaces first appeared due in part to research taking place in the early 1970s at Xerox PARC research facility. The first GUI appeared on the Xerox Alto computer in 1973. However, graphical interfaces became more widespread with the advent of Apple Macintosh computers in the 1980s. The user interface for the Macintosh operating system (Mac OS) has undergone various changes over the years, the most significant being the adoption of the *Aqua* interface that appeared with Mac OS X. Microsoft's first version of Windows—Version 1.0—was based on the addition of a GUI interface to the MS-DOS operating system. Later versions of Windows have made cosmetic changes in the appearance of the GUI along with several enhancements in its functionality, including Windows Explorer.

Traditionally, UNIX systems have been dominated by command-line interfaces. Various GUI interfaces are available, however, including the Common Desktop Environment (CDE) and X-Windows systems, which are common on commercial versions of UNIX, such as Solaris and IBM's AIX system. In addition, there has been significant development in GUI designs from various **open-source** projects, such as *K Desktop Environment* (or *KDE*) and the *GNOME* desktop by the GNU project. Both the KDE and GNOME desktops run on Linux and various UNIX systems and are available under open-source licenses, which means their source code is readily available for reading and for modification under specific license terms.

The choice of whether to use a command-line or GUI interface is mostly one of personal preference. As a very general rule, many UNIX users prefer command-line interfaces, as they often provide powerful shell interfaces. In contrast, most Windows users are pleased to use the Windows GUI environment and almost never use the MS-DOS shell interface. The various changes undergone by the Macintosh operating systems provide a nice study in contrast. Historically, Mac OS has not provided a command-line interface, always requiring its users to interface with the operating system using its GUI. However, with the release of Mac OS X (which is in part implemented using a UNIX kernel), the operating system now provides both a new Aqua interface and a command-line interface. Figure 2.3 is a screenshot of the Mac OS X GUI.

The user interface can vary from system to system and even from user to user within a system. It typically is substantially removed from the actual system structure. The design of a useful and friendly user interface is therefore

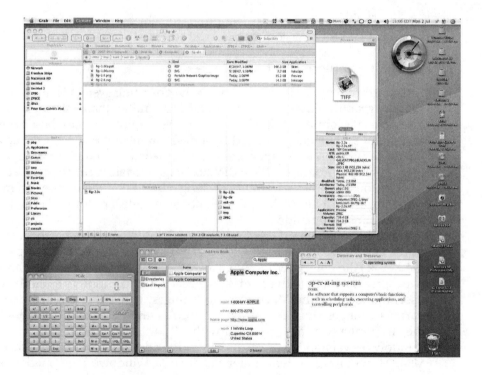

Figure 2.3   The Mac OS X GUI.

not a direct function of the operating system. In this book, we concentrate on the fundamental problems of providing adequate service to user programs. From the point of view of the operating system, we do not distinguish between user programs and system programs.

2.3 System Calls

System calls provide an interface to the services made available by an operating system. These calls are generally available as routines written in C and C++, although certain low-level tasks (for example, tasks where hardware must be accessed directly), may need to be written using assembly-language instructions.

Before we discuss how an operating system makes system calls available, let's first use an example to illustrate how system calls are used: writing a simple program to read data from one file and copy them to another file. The first input that the program will need is the names of the two files: the input file and the output file. These names can be specified in many ways, depending on the operating-system design. One approach is for the program to ask the user for the names of the two files. In an interactive system, this approach will require a sequence of system calls, first to write a prompting message on the screen and then to read from the keyboard the characters that define the two files. On mouse-based and icon-based systems, a menu of file names is usually displayed in a window. The user can then use the mouse to select the source name, and a window can be opened for the destination name to be specified. This sequence requires many I/O system calls.

Once the two file names are obtained, the program must open the input file and create the output file. Each of these operations requires another system call. There are also possible error conditions for each operation. When the program tries to open the input file, it may find that there is no file of that name or that the file is protected against access. In these cases, the program should print a message on the console (another sequence of system calls) and then terminate abnormally (another system call). If the input file exists, then we must create a new output file. We may find that there is already an output file with the same name. This situation may cause the program to abort (a system call), or we may delete the existing file (another system call) and create a new one (another system call). Another option, in an interactive system, is to ask the user (via a sequence of system calls to output the prompting message and to read the response from the terminal) whether to replace the existing file or to abort the program.

Now that both files are set up, we enter a loop that reads from the input file (a system call) and writes to the output file (another system call). Each read and write must return status information regarding various possible error conditions. On input, the program may find that the end of the file has been reached or that there was a hardware failure in the read (such as a parity error). The write operation may encounter various errors, depending on the output device (no more disk space, printer out of paper, and so on).

Finally, after the entire file is copied, the program may close both files (another system call), write a message to the console or window (more system calls), and finally terminate normally (the final system call). As we can see, even simple programs may make heavy use of the operating system. Frequently, systems execute thousands of system calls per second. This system-call sequence is shown in Figure 2.4.

Most programmers never see this level of detail, however. Typically, application developers design programs according to an **application programming interface (API)**. The API specifies a set of functions that are available to an application programmer, including the parameters that are passed to each function and the return values the programmer can expect. Three of the most common APIs available to application programmers are the Win32 API for Windows systems, the POSIX API for POSIX-based systems (which include virtually all versions of UNIX, Linux, and Mac OS X), and the Java API for designing programs that run on the Java virtual machine. Note that—unless specified—the system-call names used throughout this text are generic examples. Each operating system has its own name for each system call.

Behind the scenes, the functions that make up an API typically invoke the actual system calls on behalf of the application programmer. For example, the Win32 function `CreateProcess()` (which unsurprisingly is used to create a new process) actually calls the `NTCreateProcess()` system call in the Windows kernel. Why would an application programmer prefer programming according to an API rather than invoking actual system calls? There are several reasons for doing so. One benefit of programming according to an API concerns program portability: An application programmer designing a program using an API can expect her program to compile and run on any system that supports the same API (although in reality, architectural differences often make this more difficult than it may appear). Furthermore, actual system calls can often be more detailed and difficult to work with than the API available to an application programmer. Regardless, there often exists a strong correlation between a function in the API and its associated system call within the kernel.

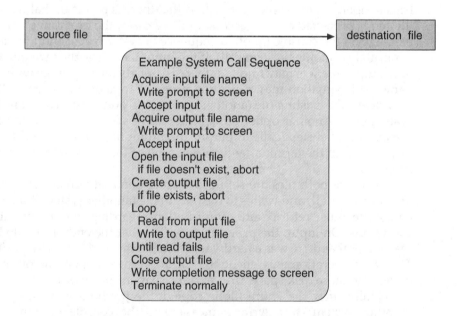

Figure 2.4 Example of how system calls are used.

EXAMPLE OF STANDARD API

As an example of a standard API, consider the ReadFile() function in the Win32 API—a function for reading from a file. The API for this function appears in Figure 2.5.

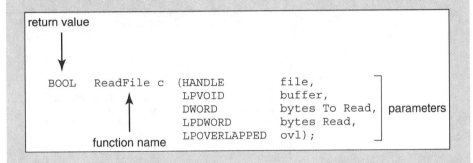

Figure 2.5   The API for the ReadFile() function.

A description of the parameters passed to ReadFile() is as follows:

- HANDLE file—the file to be read

- LPVOID buffer—a buffer where the data will be read into and written from

- DWORD bytesToRead—the number of bytes to be read into the buffer

- LPDWORD bytesRead—the number of bytes read during the last read

- LPOVERLAPPED ovl—indicates if overlapped I/O is being used

In fact, many of the POSIX and Win32 APIs are similar to the native system calls provided by the UNIX, Linux, and Windows operating systems.

The run-time support system (a set of functions built into libraries included with a compiler) for most programming languages provides a **system-call interface** that serves as the link to system calls made available by the operating system. The system-call interface intercepts function calls in the API and invokes the necessary system calls within the operating system. Typically, a number is associated with each system call, and the system-call interface maintains a table indexed according to these numbers. The system call interface then invokes the intended system call in the operating-system kernel and returns the status of the system call and any return values.

The caller need know nothing about how the system call is implemented or what it does during execution. Rather, it need only obey the API and understand what the operating system will do as a result of the execution of that system call. Thus, most of the details of the operating-system interface are hidden from the programmer by the API and are managed by the run-time support library. The relationship between an API, the system-call interface, and the operating

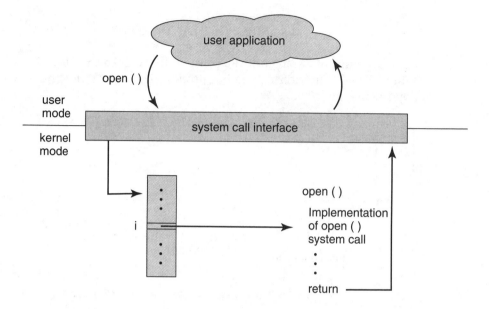

Figure 2.6   The handling of a user application invoking the open() system call.

system is shown in Figure 2.6, which illustrates how the operating system handles a user application invoking the open() system call.

System calls occur in different ways, depending on the computer in use. Often, more information is required than simply the identity of the desired system call. The exact type and amount of information vary according to the particular operating system and call. For example, to get input, we may need to specify the file or device to use as the source, as well as the address and length of the memory buffer into which the input should be read. Of course, the device or file and length may be implicit in the call.

Three general methods are used to pass parameters to the operating system. The simplest approach is to pass the parameters in *registers*. In some cases, however, there may be more parameters than registers. In these cases, the parameters are generally stored in a *block*, or table, in memory, and the address of the block is passed as a parameter in a register (Figure 2.7). This is the approach taken by Linux and Solaris. Parameters also can be placed, or *pushed*, onto the *stack* by the program and *popped* off the stack by the operating system. Some operating systems prefer the block or stack method because those approaches do not limit the number or length of parameters being passed.

2.4   Types of System Calls

System calls can be grouped roughly into six major categories: **process control, file manipulation, device manipulation, information maintenance, communications**, and **protection**. In Sections 2.4.1 through 2.4.6, we discuss briefly the types of system calls that may be provided by an operating system. Most of these system calls support, or are supported by, concepts and functions

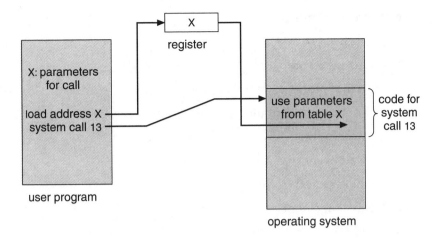

Figure 2.7   Passing of parameters as a table.

that are discussed in later chapters. Figure 2.8 summarizes the types of system calls normally provided by an operating system.

2.4.1   Process Control

A running program needs to be able to halt its execution either normally (end) or abnormally (abort). If a system call is made to terminate the currently running program abnormally, or if the program runs into a problem and causes an error trap, a dump of memory is sometimes taken and an error message generated. The dump is written to disk and may be examined by a debugger—a system program designed to aid the programmer in finding and correcting bugs—to determine the cause of the problem. Under either normal or abnormal circumstances, the operating system must transfer control to the invoking command interpreter. The command interpreter then reads the next command. In an interactive system, the command interpreter simply continues with the next command; it is assumed that the user will issue an appropriate command to respond to any error. In a GUI system, a pop-up window might alert the user to the error and ask for guidance. In a batch system, the command interpreter usually terminates the entire job and continues with the next job. Some systems allow control cards to indicate special recovery actions in case an error occurs. A control card is a batch-system concept. It is a command to manage the execution of a process. If the program discovers an error in its input and wants to terminate abnormally, it may also want to define an error level. More severe errors can be indicated by a higher-level error parameter. It is then possible to combine normal and abnormal termination by defining a normal termination as an error at level 0. The command interpreter or a following program can use this error level to determine the next action automatically.

A process or job executing one program may want to load and execute another program. This feature allows the command interpreter to execute a program as directed by, for example, a user command, the click of a mouse, or a batch command. An interesting question is where to return control when the loaded program terminates. This question is related to the problem of

- Process control
    - end, abort
    - load, execute
    - create process, terminate process
    - get process attributes, set process attributes
    - wait for time
    - wait event, signal event
    - allocate and free memory
- File management
    - create file, delete file
    - open, close
    - read, write, reposition
    - get file attributes, set file attributes
- Device management
    - request device, release device
    - read, write, reposition
    - get device attributes, set device attributes
    - logically attach or detach devices
- Information maintenance
    - get time or date, set time or date
    - get system data, set system data
    - get process, file, or device attributes
    - set process, file, or device attributes
- Communications
    - create, delete communication connection
    - send, receive messages
    - transfer status information
    - attach or detach remote devices

Figure 2.8   Types of system calls.

whether the existing program is lost, saved, or allowed to continue execution concurrently with the new program.

If control returns to the existing program when the new program terminates, we must save the memory image of the existing program; thus, we have effectively created a mechanism for one program to call another program. If both programs continue concurrently, we have created a new job or process to

EXAMPLES OF WINDOWS AND UNIX SYSTEM CALLS

	Windows	Unix
Process Control	CreateProcess() ExitProcess() WaitForSingleObject()	fork() exit() wait()
File Manipulation	CreateFile() ReadFile() WriteFile() CloseHandle()	open() read() write() close()
Device Manipulation	SetConsoleMode() ReadConsole() WriteConsole()	ioctl() read() write()
Information Maintenance	GetCurrentProcessID() SetTimer() Sleep()	getpid() alarm() sleep()
Communication	CreatePipe() CreateFileMapping() MapViewOfFile()	pipe() shmget() mmap()
Protection	SetFileSecurity() InitlializeSecurityDescriptor() SetSecurityDescriptorGroup()	chmod() umask() chown()

be multiprogrammed. Often, there is a system call specifically for this purpose (create process or submit job).

If we create a new job or process, or perhaps even a set of jobs or processes, we should be able to control its execution. This control requires the ability to determine and reset the attributes of a job or process, including the job's priority, its maximum allowable execution time, and so on (get process attributes and set process attributes). We may also want to terminate a job or process that we created (terminate process) if we find that it is incorrect or is no longer needed.

Having created new jobs or processes, we may need to wait for them to finish their execution. We may want to wait for a certain amount of time to pass (wait time); more probably, we will want to wait for a specific event to occur (wait event). The jobs or processes should then signal when that event has occurred (signal event). Quite often, two or more processes may share data. To ensure the integrity of the data being shared, operating systems often provide system calls allowing a process to **lock** shared data, thus preventing another process from accessing the data while it is locked. Typically such system calls include acquire lock and release lock. System calls of these

EXAMPLE OF STANDARD C LIBRARY

The standard C library provides a portion of the system-call interface for many versions of UNIX and Linux. As an example, let's assume a C program invokes the `printf()` statement. The C library intercepts this call and invokes the necessary system call(s) in the operating system—in this instance, the `write()` system call. The C library takes the value returned by `write()` and passes it back to the user program. This is shown in Figure 2.9.

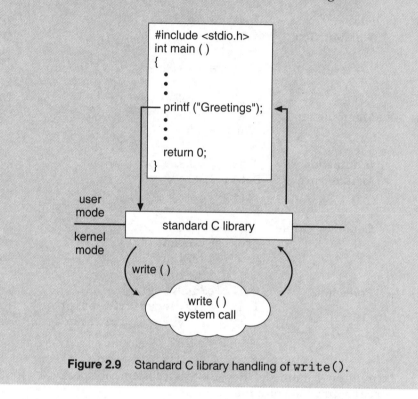

Figure 2.9   Standard C library handling of `write()`.

types, dealing with the coordination of concurrent processes, are discussed in great detail in Chapter 6.

There are so many facets of and variations in process and job control that we next use two examples—one involving a single-tasking system and the other a multitasking system—to clarify these concepts. The MS-DOS operating system is an example of a single-tasking system. It has a command interpreter that is invoked when the computer is started (Figure 2.10(a)). Because MS-DOS is single-tasking, it uses a simple method to run a program and does not create a new process. It loads the program into memory, writing over most of itself to give the program as much memory as possible (Figure 2.10(b)). Next, it sets the instruction pointer to the first instruction of the program. The program then runs, and either an error causes a trap, or the program executes a system call to terminate. In either case, the error code is saved in the system memory for later use. Following this action, the small portion of the command interpreter that was not overwritten resumes execution. Its first task is to reload the rest

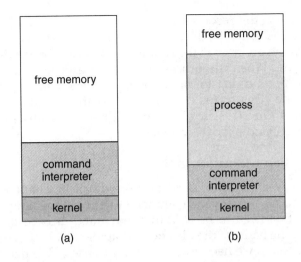

Figure 2.10 MS-DOS execution. (a) At system startup. (b) Running a program.

of the command interpreter from disk. Then the command interpreter makes the previous error code available to the user or to the next program.

FreeBSD (derived from Berkeley UNIX) is an example of a multitasking system. When a user logs on to the system, the shell of the user's choice is run. This shell is similar to the MS-DOS shell in that it accepts commands and executes programs that the user requests. However, since FreeBSD is a multitasking system, the command interpreter may continue running while another program is executed (Figure 2.11). To start a new process, the shell executes a `fork()` system call. Then, the selected program is loaded into memory via an `exec()` system call, and the program is executed. Depending on the way the command was issued, the shell then either waits for the process to finish or runs the process "in the background." In the latter case, the shell immediately requests another command. When a process is running in the background, it cannot receive input directly from the keyboard, because the

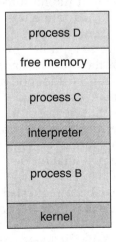

Figure 2.11 FreeBSD running multiple programs.

shell is using this resource. I/O is therefore done through files or through a GUI interface. Meanwhile, the user is free to ask the shell to run other programs, to monitor the progress of the running process, to change that program's priority, and so on. When the process is done, it executes an `exit()` system call to terminate, returning to the invoking process a status code of 0 or a nonzero error code. This status or error code is then available to the shell or other programs. Processes are discussed in Chapter 3 with a program example using the `fork()` and `exec()` system calls.

2.4.2 File Management

The file system is discussed in more detail in Chapters 10 and 11. We can, however, identify several common system calls dealing with files.

We first need to be able to `create` and `delete` files. Either system call requires the name of the file and perhaps some of the file's attributes. Once the file is created, we need to `open` it and to use it. We may also `read`, `write`, or `reposition` (rewinding or skipping to the end of the file, for example). Finally, we need to `close` the file, indicating that we are no longer using it.

We may need these same sets of operations for directories if we have a directory structure for organizing files in the file system. In addition, for either files or directories, we need to be able to determine the values of various attributes and perhaps to reset them if necessary. File attributes include the file name, file type, protection codes, accounting information, and so on. At least two system calls, `get file attribute` and `set file attribute`, are required for this function. Some operating systems provide many more calls, such as calls for file `move` and `copy`. Others might provide an API that performs those operations using code and other system calls, and others might just provide system programs to perform those tasks. If the system programs are callable by other programs, then each can be considered an API by other system programs.

2.4.3 Device Management

A process may need several resources to execute—main memory, disk drives, access to files, and so on. If the resources are available, they can be granted, and control can be returned to the user process. Otherwise, the process will have to wait until sufficient resources are available.

The various resources controlled by the operating system can be thought of as devices. Some of these devices are physical devices (for example, disk drives), while others can be thought of as abstract or virtual devices (for example, files). A system with multiple users may require us to first `request` the device, to ensure exclusive use of it. After we are finished with the device, we `release` it. These functions are similar to the `open` and `close` system calls for files. Other operating systems allow unmanaged access to devices. The hazard then is the potential for device contention and perhaps deadlock, which is described in Chapter 7.

Once the device has been requested (and allocated to us), we can `read`, `write`, and (possibly) `reposition` the device, just as we can with files. In fact, the similarity between I/O devices and files is so great that many operating systems, including UNIX, merge the two into a combined file–device structure. In this case, a set of system calls is used on both files and devices. Sometimes,

I/O devices are identified by special file names, directory placement, or file attributes.

The user interface can also make files and devices appear to be similar, even though the underlying system calls are dissimilar. This is another example of the many design decisions that go into building an operating system and user interface.

2.4.4 Information Maintenance

Many system calls exist simply for the purpose of transferring information between the user program and the operating system. For example, most systems have a system call to return the current time and date. Other system calls may return information about the system, such as the number of current users, the version number of the operating system, the amount of free memory or disk space, and so on.

Another set of system calls is helpful in debugging a program. Many systems provide system calls to dump memory. This provision is useful for debugging. A program trace lists each system call as it is executed. Even microprocessors provide a CPU mode known as *single step*, in which a trap is executed by the CPU after every instruction. The trap is usually caught by a debugger.

Many operating systems provide a time profile of a program to indicate the amount of time that the program executes at a particular location or set of locations. A time profile requires either a tracing facility or regular timer interrupts. At every occurrence of the timer interrupt, the value of the program counter is recorded. With sufficiently frequent timer interrupts, a statistical picture of the time spent on various parts of the program can be obtained.

In addition, the operating system keeps information about all its processes, and system calls are used to access this information. Generally, calls are also used to reset the process information (get process attributes and set process attributes). In Section 3.1.3, we discuss what information is normally kept.

2.4.5 Communication

There are two common models of interprocess communication: the message-passing model and the shared-memory model. In the **message-passing model**, the communicating processes exchange messages with one another to transfer information. Messages can be exchanged between the processes either directly or indirectly through a common mailbox. Before communication can take place, a connection must be opened. The name of the other communicator must be known, be it another process on the same system or a process on another computer connected by a communications network. Each computer in a network has a *host name* by which it is commonly known. A host also has a network identifier, such as an IP address. Similarly, each process has a *process name*, and this name is translated into an identifier by which the operating system can refer to the process. The get hostid and get processid system calls do this translation. The identifiers are then passed to the general-purpose open and close calls provided by the file system or to specific open connection and close connection system calls, depending on the system's model of communication. The recipient process usually must give its permission for communication to take place with an `accept connection` call. Most processes that will be receiving connections are special-purpose *daemons*, which are systems programs provided for that purpose. They execute a `wait for connection` call and are awakened when a connection is made. The source of the communication, known as the *client,* and the receiving daemon, known as a *server,* then exchange messages by using `read message` and `write message` system calls. The `close connection` call terminates the communication.

In the **shared-memory model**, processes use `shared memory create` and `shared memory attach` system calls to create and gain access to regions of memory owned by other processes. Recall that, normally, the operating system tries to prevent one process from accessing another process's memory. Shared memory requires that two or more processes agree to remove this restriction. They can then exchange information by reading and writing data in the shared areas. The form of the data is determined by the processes and are not under the operating system's control. The processes are also responsible for ensuring that they are not writing to the same location simultaneously. Such mechanisms are discussed in Chapter 6. In Chapter 4, we look at a variation of the process scheme—threads—in which memory is shared by default.

Both of the models just discussed are common in operating systems, and most systems implement both. Message passing is useful for exchanging smaller amounts of data, because no conflicts need be avoided. It is also easier to implement than is shared memory for intercomputer communication. Shared memory allows maximum speed and convenience of communication, since it can be done at memory transfer speeds when it takes place within a computer. Problems exist, however, in the areas of protection and synchronization between the processes sharing memory.

2.4.6 Protection

Protection provides a mechanism for controlling access to the resources provided by a computer system. Historically, protection was a concern only on multiprogrammed computer systems with several users. However, with the advent of networking and the Internet, all computer systems, from servers to PDAs, must be concerned with protection.

Typically, system calls providing protection include `set permission` and `get permission`, which manipulate the permission settings of resources such as files and disks. The `allow user` and `deny user` system calls specify whether particular users can—or cannot—be allowed access to certain resources.

We cover protection in Chapter 14 and the much larger issue of security in Chapter 15.

2.5 System Programs

Another aspect of a modern system is the collection of system programs. Recall Figure 1.1, which depicted the logical computer hierarchy. At the lowest level is hardware. Next is the operating system, then the system programs, and finally the application programs. **System programs**, also known as **system utilities**, provide a convenient environment for program development and execution.

Some of them are simply user interfaces to system calls; others are considerably more complex. They can be divided into these categories:

- **File management**. These programs create, delete, copy, rename, print, dump, list, and generally manipulate files and directories.

- **Status information**. Some programs simply ask the system for the date, time, amount of available memory or disk space, number of users, or similar status information. Others are more complex, providing detailed performance, logging, and debugging information. Typically, these programs format and print the output to the terminal or other output devices or files or display it in a window of the GUI. Some systems also support a registry, which is used to store and retrieve configuration information.

- **File modification**. Several text editors may be available to create and modify the content of files stored on disk or other storage devices. There may also be special commands to search contents of files or perform transformations of the text.

- **Programming-language support**. Compilers, assemblers, debuggers, and interpreters for common programming languages (such as C, C++, Java, Visual Basic, and PERL) are often provided to the user with the operating system.

- **Program loading and execution**. Once a program is assembled or compiled, it must be loaded into memory to be executed. The system may provide absolute loaders, relocatable loaders, linkage editors, and overlay loaders. Debugging systems for either higher-level languages or machine language are needed as well.

- **Communications**. These programs provide the mechanism for creating virtual connections among processes, users, and computer systems. They allow users to send messages to one another's screens, to browse Web pages, to send electronic-mail messages, to log in remotely, or to transfer files from one machine to another.

In addition to systems programs, most operating systems are supplied with programs that are useful in solving common problems or performing common operations. Such **application programs** include Web browsers, word processors and text formatters, spreadsheets, database systems, compilers, plotting and statistical-analysis packages, and games.

The view of the operating system seen by most users is defined by the application and system programs, rather than by the actual system calls. Consider a user's PC. When a user's computer is running the Mac OS X operating system, the user might see the GUI, featuring a mouse-and-windows interface. Alternatively, or even in one of the windows, the user might have a command-line UNIX shell. Both use the same set of system calls, but the system calls look different and act in different ways. Further confusing the user view, consider the user dual-booting from Mac OS X into Windows Vista. Now the same user on the same hardware has two entirely different interfaces and two sets of applications using the same physical resources. On the same hardware, then, a user can be exposed to multiple user interfaces sequentially or concurrently.

2.6   Operating-System Design and Implementation

In this section, we discuss problems we face in designing and implementing an operating system. There are, of course, no complete solutions to such problems, but there are approaches that have proved successful.

2.6.1   Design Goals

The first problem in designing a system is to define goals and specifications. At the highest level, the design of the system will be affected by the choice of hardware and the type of system: batch, time shared, single user, multiuser, distributed, real time, or general purpose.

Beyond this highest design level, the requirements may be much harder to specify. The requirements can, however, be divided into two basic groups: *user* goals and *system* goals.

Users desire certain obvious properties in a system. The system should be convenient to use, easy to learn and to use, reliable, safe, and fast. Of course, these specifications are not particularly useful in the system design, since there is no general agreement on how to achieve them.

A similar set of requirements can be defined by those people who must design, create, maintain, and operate the system. The system should be easy to design, implement, and maintain; and it should be flexible, reliable, error free, and efficient. Again, these requirements are vague and may be interpreted in various ways.

There is, in short, no unique solution to the problem of defining the requirements for an operating system. The wide range of systems in existence shows that different requirements can result in a large variety of solutions for different environments. For example, the requirements for VxWorks, a real-time operating system for embedded systems, must have been substantially different from those for MVS, a large multiuser, multiaccess operating system for IBM mainframes.

Specifying and designing an operating system is a highly creative task. Although no textbook can tell you how to do it, general principles have been developed in the field of **software engineering**, and we turn now to a discussion of some of these principles.

2.6.2   Mechanisms and Policies

One important principle is the separation of **policy** from **mechanism**. Mechanisms determine *how* to do something; policies determine *what* will be done. For example, the timer construct (see Section 1.5.2) is a mechanism for ensuring CPU protection, but deciding how long the timer is to be set for a particular user is a policy decision.

The separation of policy and mechanism is important for flexibility. Policies are likely to change across places or over time. In the worst case, each change in policy would require a change in the underlying mechanism. A general mechanism insensitive to changes in policy would be more desirable. A change in policy would then require redefinition of only certain parameters of the system. For instance, consider a mechanism for giving priority to certain types of programs over others. If the mechanism is properly separated from policy, it can be used either to support a policy decision that I/O-intensive programs should have priority over CPU-intensive ones or to support the opposite policy.

Microkernel-based operating systems (Section 2.7.3) take the separation of mechanism and policy to one extreme by implementing a basic set of primitive building blocks. These blocks are almost policy free, allowing more advanced mechanisms and policies to be added via user-created kernel modules or via user programs themselves. As an example, consider the history of UNIX. At first, it had a time-sharing scheduler. In the latest version of Solaris, scheduling is controlled by loadable tables. Depending on the table currently loaded, the system can be time shared, batch processing, real time, fair share, or any combination. Making the scheduling mechanism general purpose allows vast policy changes to be made with a single load-new-table command. At the other extreme is a system such as Windows, in which both mechanism and policy are encoded in the system to enforce a global look and feel. All applications have similar interfaces, because the interface itself is built into the kernel and system libraries. The Mac OS X operating system has similar functionality.

Policy decisions are important for all resource allocation. Whenever it is necessary to decide whether or not to allocate a resource, a policy decision must be made. Whenever the question is *how* rather than *what*, it is a mechanism that must be determined.

2.6.3 Implementation

Once an operating system is designed, it must be implemented. Traditionally, operating systems have been written in assembly language. Now, however, they are most commonly written in higher-level languages such as C or C++.

The first system that was not written in assembly language was probably the Master Control Program (MCP) for Burroughs computers. MCP was written in a variant of ALGOL. MULTICS, developed at MIT, was written mainly in PL/1. The Linux and Windows XP operating systems are written mostly in C, although there are some small sections of assembly code for device drivers and for saving and restoring the state of registers.

The advantages of using a higher-level language, or at least a systems-implementation language, for implementing operating systems are the same as those accrued when the language is used for application programs: the code can be written faster, is more compact, and is easier to understand and debug. In addition, improvements in compiler technology will improve the generated code for the entire operating system by simple recompilation. Finally, an operating system is far easier to *port*—to move to some other hardware—if it is written in a higher-level language. For example, MS-DOS was written in Intel 8088 assembly language. Consequently, it runs natively only on the Intel X86 family of CPUs. (Although MS-DOS runs natively only on Intel X86, emulators of the X86 instruction set allow the operating system to run non-natively—slower, with more resource use—on other CPUs. Emulators are programs that duplicate the functionality of one system with another system.) The Linux operating system, in contrast, is written mostly in C and is available natively on a number of different CPUs, including Intel X86, Sun SPARC, and IBMPowerPC.

The only possible disadvantages of implementing an operating system in a higher-level language are reduced speed and increased storage requirements. This, however, is no longer a major issue in today's systems. Although an expert assembly-language programmer can produce efficient small routines, for large programs a modern compiler can perform complex analysis and apply sophisticated optimizations that produce excellent code. Modern processors have deep pipelining and multiple functional units that can handle the details of complex dependencies much more easily than can the human mind.

As is true in other systems, major performance improvements in operating systems are more likely to be the result of better data structures and algorithms than of excellent assembly-language code. In addition, although operating systems are large, only a small amount of the code is critical to high performance; the memory manager and the CPU scheduler are probably the most critical routines. After the system is written and is working correctly, bottleneck routines can be identified and can be replaced with assembly-language equivalents.

2.7   Operating-System Structure

A system as large and complex as a modern operating system must be engineered carefully if it is to function properly and be modified easily. A common approach is to partition the task into small components rather than have one monolithic system. Each of these modules should be a well-defined portion of the system, with carefully defined inputs, outputs, and functions. We have already discussed briefly in Chapter 1 the common components of operating systems. In this section, we discuss how these components are interconnected and melded into a kernel.

2.7.1   Simple Structure

Many commercial operating systems do not have well-defined structures. Frequently, such systems started as small, simple, and limited systems and then grew beyond their original scope. MS-DOS is an example of such a system. It was originally designed and implemented by a few people who had no idea that it would become so popular. It was written to provide the most functionality in the least space, so it was not divided into modules carefully. Figure 2.12 shows its structure.

In MS-DOS, the interfaces and levels of functionality are not well separated. For instance, application programs are able to access the basic I/O routines to write directly to the display and disk drives. Such freedom leaves MS-DOS vulnerable to errant (or malicious) programs, causing entire system crashes when user programs fail. Of course, MS-DOS was also limited by the hardware of its era. Because the Intel 8088 for which it was written provides no dual mode and no hardware protection, the designers of MS-DOS had no choice but to leave the base hardware accessible.

Another example of limited structuring is the original UNIX operating system. Like MS-DOS, UNIX initially was limited by hardware functionality. It consists of two separable parts: the kernel and the system programs. The kernel

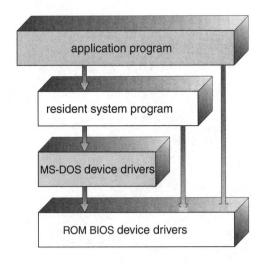

Figure 2.12 MS-DOS layer structure.

is further separated into a series of interfaces and device drivers, which have been added and expanded over the years as UNIX has evolved. We can view the traditional UNIX operating system as being layered, as shown in Figure 2.13. Everything below the system-call interface and above the physical hardware is the kernel. The kernel provides the file system, CPU scheduling, memory management, and other operating-system functions through system calls. Taken in sum, that is an enormous amount of functionality to be combined into one level. This monolithic structure was difficult to implement and maintain.

2.7.2 Layered Approach

With proper hardware support, operating systems can be broken into pieces that are smaller and more appropriate than those allowed by the original

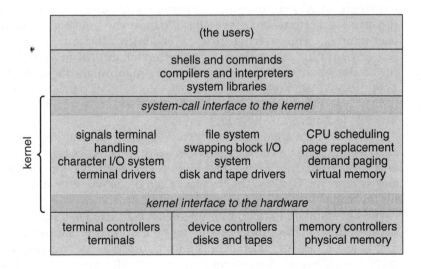

Figure 2.13 Traditional UNIX system structure.

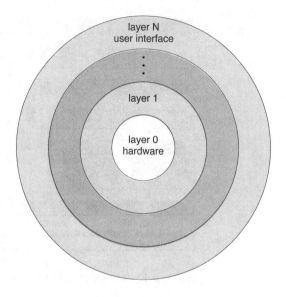

Figure 2.14   A layered operating system.

MS-DOS and UNIX systems. The operating system can then retain much greater control over the computer and over the applications that make use of that computer. Implementers have more freedom in changing the inner workings of the system and in creating modular operating systems. Under a top-down approach, the overall functionality and features are determined and are separated into components. Information hiding is also important, because it leaves programmers free to implement the low-level routines as they see fit, provided that the external interface of the routine stays unchanged and that the routine itself performs the advertised task.

A system can be made modular in many ways. One method is the **layered approach**, in which the operating system is broken into a number of layers (levels). The bottom layer (layer 0) is the hardware; the highest (layer N) is the user interface. This layering structure is depicted in Figure 2.14.

An operating-system layer is an implementation of an abstract object made up of data and the operations that can manipulate those data. A typical operating-system layer—say, layer M—consists of data structures and a set of routines that can be invoked by higher-level layers. Layer M, in turn, can invoke operations on lower-level layers.

The main advantage of the layered approach is simplicity of construction and debugging. The layers are selected so that each uses functions (operations) and services of only lower-level layers. This approach simplifies debugging and system verification. The first layer can be debugged without any concern for the rest of the system, because, by definition, it uses only the basic hardware (which is assumed correct) to implement its functions. Once the first layer is debugged, its correct functioning can be assumed while the second layer is debugged, and so on. If an error is found during the debugging of a particular layer, the error must be on that layer, because the layers below it are already debugged. Thus, the design and implementation of the system are simplified.

Each layer is implemented with only those operations provided by lower-level layers. A layer does not need to know how these operations are implemented; it needs to know only what these operations do. Hence, each layer hides the existence of certain data structures, operations, and hardware from higher-level layers.

The major difficulty with the layered approach involves appropriately defining the various layers. Because a layer can use only lower-level layers, careful planning is necessary. For example, the device driver for the backing store (disk space used by virtual-memory algorithms) must be at a lower level than the memory-management routines, because memory management requires the ability to use the backing store.

Other requirements may not be so obvious. The backing-store driver would normally be above the CPU scheduler, because the driver may need to wait for I/O and the CPU can be rescheduled during this time. However, on a large system, the CPU scheduler may have more information about all the active processes than can fit in memory. Therefore, this information may need to be swapped in and out of memory, requiring the backing-store driver routine to be below the CPU scheduler.

A final problem with layered implementations is that they tend to be less efficient than other types. For instance, when a user program executes an I/O operation, it executes a system call that is trapped to the I/O layer, which calls the memory-management layer, which in turn calls the CPU-scheduling layer, which is then passed to the hardware. At each layer, the parameters may be modified, data may need to be passed, and so on. Each layer adds overhead to the system call; the net result is a system call that takes longer than does one on a nonlayered system.

These limitations have caused a small backlash against layering in recent years. Fewer layers with more functionality are being designed, providing most of the advantages of modularized code while avoiding the difficult problems of layer definition and interaction.

2.7.3 Microkernels

We have already seen that as UNIX expanded, the kernel became large and difficult to manage. In the mid-1980s, researchers at Carnegie Mellon University developed an operating system called **Mach** that modularized the kernel using the **microkernel** approach. This method structures the operating system by removing all nonessential components from the kernel and implementing them as system and user-level programs. The result is a smaller kernel. There is little consensus regarding which services should remain in the kernel and which should be implemented in user space. Typically, however, microkernels provide minimal process and memory management, in addition to a communication facility.

The main function of the microkernel is to provide a communication facility between the client program and the various services that are also running in user space. Communication is provided by *message passing*, which was described in Section 2.4.5. For example, if the client program wishes to access a file, it must interact with the file server. The client program and service never interact directly. Rather, they communicate indirectly by exchanging messages with the microkernel.

One benefit of the microkernel approach is ease of extending the operating system. All new services are added to user space and consequently do not require modification of the kernel. When the kernel does have to be modified, the changes tend to be fewer, because the microkernel is a smaller kernel. The resulting operating system is easier to port from one hardware design to another. The microkernel also provides more security and reliability, since most services are running as user—rather than kernel—processes. If a service fails, the rest of the operating system remains untouched.

Several contemporary operating systems have used the microkernel approach. Tru64 UNIX (formerly Digital UNIX) provides a UNIX interface to the user, but it is implemented with a Mach kernel. The Mach kernel maps UNIX system calls into messages to the appropriate user-level services. The Mac OS X kernel (also known as *Darwin*) is also based on the Mach microkernel.

Another example is QNX, a real-time operating system. The QNX micro-kernel provides services for message passing and process scheduling. It also handles low-level network communication and hardware interrupts. All other services in QNX are provided by standard processes that run outside the kernel in user mode.

Unfortunately, microkernels can suffer from performance decreases due to increased system function overhead. Consider the history of Windows NT. The first release had a layered microkernel organization. However, this version delivered low performance compared with that of Windows 95. Windows NT 4.0 partially redressed the performance problem by moving layers from user space to kernel space and integrating them more closely. By the time Windows XP was designed, its architecture was more monolithic than microkernel.

2.7.4 Modules

Perhaps the best current methodology for operating-system design involves using object-oriented programming techniques to create a modular kernel. Here, the kernel has a set of core components and links in additional services either during boot time or during run time. Such a strategy uses dynamically loadable modules and is common in modern implementations of UNIX, such as Solaris, Linux, and Mac OS X. For example, the Solaris operating system structure, shown in Figure 2.15, is organized around a core kernel with seven types of loadable kernel modules:

1. Scheduling classes

2. File systems

3. Loadable system calls

4. Executable formats

5. STREAMS modules

6. Miscellaneous

7. Device and bus drivers

Such a design allows the kernel to provide core services yet also allows certain features to be implemented dynamically. For example, device and

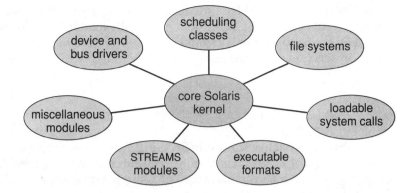

Figure 2.15 Solaris loadable modules.

bus drivers for specific hardware can be added to the kernel, and support for different file systems can be added as loadable modules. The overall result resembles a layered system in that each kernel section has defined, protected interfaces; but it is more flexible than a layered system in that any module can call any other module. Furthermore, the approach is like the microkernel approach in that the primary module has only core functions and knowledge of how to load and communicate with other modules; but it is more efficient, because modules do not need to invoke message passing in order to communicate.

The Apple Mac OS X operating system uses a hybrid structure. It is a layered system in which one layer consists of the Mach microkernel. The structure of Mac OS X appears in Figure 2.16. The top layers include application environments and a set of services providing a graphical interface to applications. Below these layers is the kernel environment, which consists primarily of the Mach microkernel and the BSD kernel. Mach provides memory management; support for remote procedure calls (RPCs) and interprocess communication (IPC) facilities, including message passing; and thread scheduling. The BSD component provides a BSD command line interface, support for networking and file systems, and an implementation of POSIX APIs, including Pthreads.

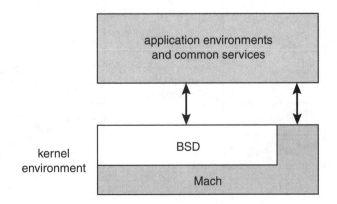

Figure 2.16 The Mac OS X structure.

In addition to Mach and BSD, the kernel environment provides an I/O kit for development of device drivers and dynamically loadable modules (which Mac OS X refers to as **kernel extensions**). As shown in the figure, applications and common services can make use of either the Mach or BSD facilities directly.

2.8 Virtual Machines

The layered approach described in Section 2.7.2 is taken to its logical conclusion in the concept of a virtual machine. The fundamental idea behind a virtual machine is to abstract the hardware of a single computer (the CPU, memory, disk drives, network interface cards, and so forth) into several different execution environments, thereby creating the illusion that each separate execution environment is running its own private computer.

By using CPU scheduling (Chapter 5) and virtual-memory techniques (Chapter 9), an operating system host can create the illusion that a process has its own processor with its own (virtual) memory. The virtual machine provides an interface that is *identical* to the underlying bare hardware. Each guest process is provided with a (virtual) copy of the underlying computer (Figure 2.17). Usually, the guest process is in fact an operating system, and that is how a single physical machine can run multiple operating systems concurrently, each in its own virtual machine.

2.8.1 History

Virtual machines first appeared commercially on IBM mainframes via the VM operating system in 1972. VM has evolved and is still available, and many of

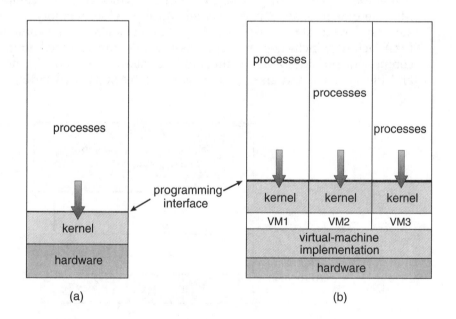

Figure 2.17   System models. (a) Nonvirtual machine. (b) Virtual machine.

the original concepts are found in other systems, making this facility worth exploring.

IBM VM370 divided a mainframe into multiple virtual machines, each running its own operating system. A major difficulty with the VM virtual-machine approach involved disk systems. Suppose that the physical machine had three disk drives but wanted to support seven virtual machines. Clearly, it could not allocate a disk drive to each virtual machine, because the virtual-machine software itself needed substantial disk space to provide virtual memory and spooling. The solution was to provide virtual disks—termed *minidisks* in IBM's VM operating system—that are identical in all respects except size. The system implemented each minidisk by allocating as many tracks on the physical disks as the minidisk needed.

Once these virtual machines were created, users could run any of the operating systems or software packages that were available on the underlying machine. For the IBM VM system, a user normally ran CMS—a single-user interactive operating system.

2.8.2   Benefits

There are several reasons for creating a virtual machine. Most of them are fundamentally related to being able to share the same hardware yet run several different execution environments (that is, different operating systems) concurrently.

One important advantage is that the host system is protected from the virtual machines, just as the virtual machines are protected from each other. A virus inside a guest operating system might damage that operating system but is unlikely to affect the host or the other guests. Because each virtual machine is completely isolated from all other virtual machines, there are no protection problems. At the same time, however, there is no direct sharing of resources. Two approaches to provide sharing have been implemented. First, it is possible to share a file-system volume and thus to share files. Second, it is possible to define a network of virtual machines, each of which can send information over the virtual communications network. The network is modeled after physical communication networks but is implemented in software.

A virtual-machine system is a perfect vehicle for operating-systems research and development. Normally, changing an operating system is a difficult task. Operating systems are large and complex programs, and it is difficult to be sure that a change in one part will not cause obscure bugs to appear in some other part. The power of the operating system makes changing it particularly dangerous. Because the operating system executes in kernel mode, a wrong change in a pointer could cause an error that would destroy the entire file system. Thus, it is necessary to test all changes to the operating system carefully.

The operating system, however, runs on and controls the entire machine. Therefore, the current system must be stopped and taken out of use while changes are made and tested. This period is commonly called *system-development time*. Since it makes the system unavailable to users, system-development time is often scheduled late at night or on weekends, when system load is low.

A virtual-machine system can eliminate much of this problem. System programmers are given their own virtual machine, and system development is done on the virtual machine instead of on a physical machine. Normal system operation seldom needs to be disrupted for system development.

Another advantage of virtual machines for developers is that multiple operating systems can be running on the developer's workstation concurrently. This virtualized workstation allows for rapid porting and testing of programs in varying environments. Similarly, quality-assurance engineers can test their applications in multiple environments without buying, powering, and maintaining a computer for each environment.

A major advantage of virtual machines in production data-center use is system consolidation, which involves taking two or more separate systems and running them in virtual machines on one system. Such physical-to-virtual conversions result in resource optimization, as many lightly used systems can be combined to create one more heavily used system.

If the use of virtual machines continues to spread, application deployment will evolve accordingly. If a system can easily add, remove, and move a virtual machine, then why install applications on that system directly? Instead, application developers would pre-install the application on a tuned and customized operating system in a virtual machine. That virtual environment would be the release mechanism for the application. This method would be an improvement for application developers; application management would become easier, less tuning would required, and technical support of the application would be more straightforward. System administrators would find the environment easier to manage as well. Installation would be simple, and redeploying the application to another system would be much easier than the usual steps of uninstalling and reinstalling. For widespread adoption of this methodology to occur, though, the format of virtual machines must be standardized so that any virtual machine will run on any virtualization platform. The "Open Virtual Machine Format" is an attempt to do just that, and it could succeed in unifying virtual-machine formats.

2.8.3 Simulation

System virtualization as discussed so far is just one of many system-emulation methodologies. Virtualization is the most common because it makes guest operating systems and applications "believe" they are running on native hardware. Because only the system's resources need to be virtualized, these guests run at almost full speed.

Another methodology is simulation, in which the host system has one system architecture and the guest system was compiled for a different architecture. For example, suppose a company has replaced its outdated computer system with a new system but would like to continue to run certain important programs that were compiled for the old system. The programs could be run in an emulator that translates each of the outdated system's instructions into the native instruction set of the new system. Emulation can increase the life of programs and allow us to explore old architectures without having an actual old machine, but its major challenge is performance. Instruction-set emulation can run an order of magnitude slower than native instructions. Thus, unless the new machine is ten times faster than the old, the program running on the new machine will run slower than it did on its native hardware. Another challenge is that it is difficult to create a correct emulator because, in essence, this involves writing an entire CPU in software.

2.8.4 Para-virtualization

Para-virtualization is another variation on this theme. Rather than try to trick a guest operating system into believing it has a system to itself, para-virtualization presents the guest with a system that is similar but not identical to the guest's preferred system. The guest must be modified to run on the paravirtualized hardware. The gain for this extra work is more efficient use of resources and a smaller virtualization layer.

Solaris 10 includes **containers**, or **zones**, that create a virtual layer between the operating system and the applications. In this system, only one kernel is installed, and the hardware is not virtualized. Rather, the operating system and its devices are virtualized, providing processes within a container with the impression that they are the only processes on the system. One or more containers can be created, and each can have its own applications, network stacks, network address and ports, user accounts, and so on. CPU resources can be divided up among the containers and the systemwide processes. Figure 2.18 shows a Solaris 10 system with two containers and the standard "global" user space.

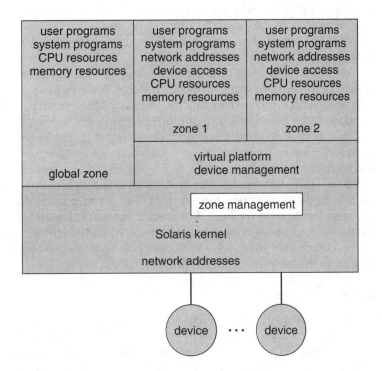

Figure 2.18 Solaris 10 with two containers.

2.8.5 Implementation

Although the virtual-machine concept is useful, it is difficult to implement. Much work is required to provide an *exact* duplicate of the underlying machine. Remember that the underlying machine typically has two modes: user mode and kernel mode. The virtual-machine software can run in kernel mode, since it is the operating system. The virtual machine itself can execute in only user mode. Just as the physical machine has two modes, however, so must the virtual machine. Consequently, we must have a virtual user mode and a virtual kernel mode, both of which run in a physical user mode. Those actions that cause a transfer from user mode to kernel mode on a real machine (such as a system call or an attempt to execute a privileged instruction) must also cause a transfer from virtual user mode to virtual kernel mode on a virtual machine.

Such a transfer can be accomplished as follows. When a system call, for example, is made by a program running on a virtual machine in virtual user mode, it will cause a transfer to the virtual-machine monitor in the real machine. When the virtual-machine monitor gains control, it can change the register contents and program counter for the virtual machine to simulate the effect of the system call. It can then restart the virtual machine, noting that it is now in virtual kernel mode.

The major difference, of course, is time. Whereas the real I/O might have taken 100 milliseconds, the virtual I/O might take less time (because it is spooled) or more time (because it is interpreted). In addition, the CPU is being multiprogrammed among many virtual machines, further slowing down the virtual machines in unpredictable ways. In the extreme case, it may be necessary to simulate all instructions to provide a true virtual machine. VM, discussed earlier, works for IBM machines because normal instructions for the virtual machines can execute directly on the hardware. Only the privileged instructions (needed mainly for I/O) must be simulated and hence execute more slowly.

Without some level of hardware support, virtualization would be impossible. The more hardware support available within a system, the more feature rich, stable, and well performing the virtual machines can be. All major general-purpose CPUs provide some amount of hardware support for virtualization. For example, AMD virtualization technology is found in several AMD processors. It defines two new modes of operation—host and guest. Virtual machine software can enable host mode, define the characteristics of each guest virtual machine, and then switch the system to guest mode, passing control of the system to the guest operating system that is running in the virtual machine. In guest mode, the virtualized operating system thinks it is running on native hardware and sees certain devices (those included in the host's definition of the guest). If the guest tries to access a virtualized resource, then control is passed to the host to manage that interaction.

2.8.6 Examples

Despite the advantages of virtual machines, they received little attention for a number of years after they were first developed. Today, however, virtual machines are coming into fashion as a means of solving system compatibility problems. In this section, we explore two popular contemporary virtual machines: the VMware Workstation and the Java virtual machine. As you will see, these virtual machines can typically run on top of operating systems of any of the design types discussed earlier. Thus, operating system design methods—simple layers, microkernels, modules, and virtual machines—are not mutually exclusive.

2.8.6.1   VMware

Most of the virtualization techniques discussed in this section require virtualization to be supported by the kernel. Another method involves writing the virtualization tool to run in user mode as an application on top of the operating system. Virtual machines running within this tool believe they are running on bare hardware but in fact are running inside a user-level application.

VMware Workstation is a popular commercial application that abstracts Intel X86 and compatible hardware into isolated virtual machines. VMware Workstation runs as an application on a host operating system such as Windows or Linux and allows this host system to concurrently run several different guest operating systems as independent virtual machines.

The architecture of such a system is shown in Figure 2.19. In this scenario, Linux is running as the host operating system; and FreeBSD, Windows NT, and Windows XP are running as guest operating systems. The virtualization layer is the heart of VMware, as it abstracts the physical hardware into isolated virtual machines running as guest operating systems. Each virtual machine has its own virtual CPU, memory, disk drives, network interfaces, and so forth.

The physical disk the guest owns and manages is really just a file within the file system of the host operating system. To create an identical guest instance, we can simply copy the file. Copying the file to another location protects the guest instance against a disaster at the original site. Moving the file to another

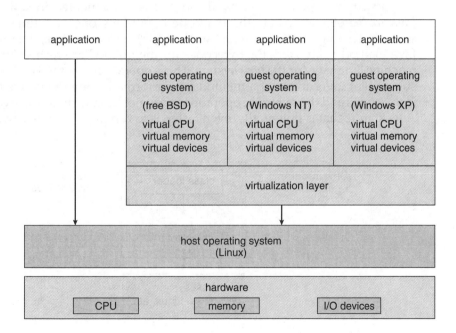

Figure 2.19   VMware architecture.

location moves the guest system. These scenarios show how virtualization can improve the efficiency of system administration as well as system resource use.

2.8.6.2   The Java Virtual Machine

Java is a popular object-oriented programming language introduced by Sun Microsystems in 1995. In addition to a language specification and a large API library, Java also provides a specification for a Java virtual machine—or JVM.

Java objects are specified with the `class` construct; a Java program consists of one or more classes. For each Java class, the compiler produces an architecture-neutral **bytecode** output (`.class`) file that will run on any implementation of the JVM.

The JVM is a specification for an abstract computer. It consists of a **class loader** and a Java interpreter that executes the architecture-neutral bytecodes, as diagrammed in Figure 2.20. The class loader loads the compiled `.class` files from both the Java program and the Java API for execution by the Java interpreter. After a class is loaded, the verifier checks that the `.class` file is valid Java bytecode and does not overflow or underflow the stack. It also ensures that the bytecode does not perform pointer arithmetic, which could provide illegal memory access. If the class passes verification, it is run by the Java interpreter. The JVM also automatically manages memory by performing **garbage collection**—the practice of reclaiming memory from objects no longer in use and returning it to the system. Much research focuses on garbage collection algorithms for increasing the performance of Java programs in the virtual machine.

The JVM may be implemented in software on top of a host operating system, such as Windows, Linux, or Mac OS X, or as part of a Web browser. Alternatively, the JVM may be implemented in hardware on a chip specifically designed to run Java programs. If the JVM is implemented in software, the Java interpreter interprets the bytecode operations one at a time. A faster software technique is to use a **just-in-time (JIT)** compiler. Here, the first time a Java method is invoked, the bytecodes for the method are turned into native machine language for the host system. These operations are then cached so that subsequent invocations of a method are performed using the native machine instructions and the bytecode operations need not be interpreted all over again. A technique that is potentially even faster is to run the JVM in hardware on a

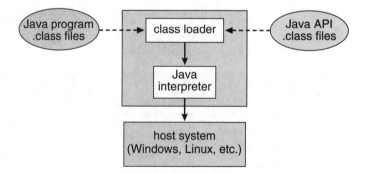

Figure 2.20   The Java virtual machine.

THE .NET FRAMEWORK

The .NET Framework is a collection of technologies, including a set of class libraries, and an execution environment that come together to provide a platform for developing software. This platform allows programs to be written to target the .NET Framework instead of a specific architecture. A program written for the .NET Framework need not worry about the specifics of the hardware or the operating system on which it will run. Thus, any architecture implementing .NET will be able to successfully execute the program. This is because the execution environment abstracts these details and provides a virtual machine as an intermediary between the executing program and the underlying architecture.

At the core of the .NET Framework is the Common Language Runtime (CLR). The CLR is the implementation of the .NET virtual machine. It provides an environment for execution of programs written in any of the languages targeted at the .NET Framework. Programs written in languages such as C# (pronounced *C-sharp*) and VB.NET are compiled into an intermediate, architecture-independent language called Microsoft Intermediate Language (MS-IL). These compiled files, called assemblies, include MS-IL instructions and metadata. They have file extensions of either .EXE or .DLL. Upon execution of a program, the CLR loads assemblies into what is known as the **Application Domain**. As instructions are requested by the executing program, the CLR converts the MS-IL instructions inside the assemblies into native code that is specific to the underlying architecture using just-in-time compilation. Once instructions have been converted to native code, they are kept and will continue to run as native code for the CPU. The architecture of the CLR for the .NET framework is shown in Figure 2.21.

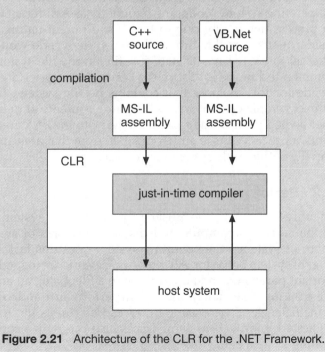

Figure 2.21 Architecture of the CLR for the .NET Framework.

special Java chip that executes the Java bytecode operations as native code, thus bypassing the need for either a software interpreter or a just-in-time compiler.

2.9   Operating-System Debugging

Broadly, **debugging** is the activity of finding and fixing errors, or **bugs**, in a system. Debugging seeks to find and fix errors in both hardware and software. Performance problems are considered bugs, so debugging can also include **performance tuning**, which seeks to improve performance by removing **bottlenecks** in the processing taking place within a system. A discussion of hardware debugging is outside of the scope of this text. In this section, we explore debugging kernel and process errors and performance problems.

2.9.1   Failure Analysis

If a process fails, most operating systems write the error information to a **log file** to alert system operators or users that the problem occurred. The operating system can also take a **core dump**—a capture of the memory (referred to as the "core" in the early days of computing) of the process. This core image is stored in a file for later analysis. Running programs and core dumps can be probed by a **debugger**, a tool designed to allow a programmer to explore the code and memory of a process.

Debugging user-level process code is a challenge. Operating system kernel debugging even more complex because of the size and complexity of the kernel, its control of the hardware, and the lack of user-level debugging tools. A kernel failure is called a **crash**. As with a process failure, error information is saved to a log file, and the memory state is saved to a **crash dump**.

Operating system debugging frequently uses different tools and techniques than process debugging due to the very different nature of these two tasks. Consider that a kernel failure in the file-system code would make it risky for the kernel to try to save its state to a file on the file system before rebooting. A common technique is to save the kernel's memory state to a section of disk set aside for this purpose that contains no file system. If the kernel detects an unrecoverable error, it writes the entire contents of memory, or at least the kernel-owned parts of the system memory, to the disk area. When the system reboots, a process runs to gather the data from that area and write it to a crash dump file within a file system for analysis.

2.9.2   Performance Tuning

To identify bottlenecks, we must be able to monitor system performance. Code must be added to compute and display measures of system behavior. In a number of systems, the operating system does this task by producing trace listings of system behavior. All interesting events are logged with their time and important parameters and are written to a file. Later, an analysis program can process the log file to determine system performance and to identify bottlenecks and inefficiencies. These same traces can be run as input for a simulation of a suggested improved system. Traces also can help people to find errors in operating-system behavior.

Kernighan's Law

"Debugging is twice as hard as writing the code in the first place. Therefore, if you write the code as cleverly as possible, you are, by definition, not smart enough to debug it."

Another approach to performance tuning is to include interactive tools with the system that allow users and administrators to question the state of various components of the system to look for bottlenecks. The UNIX command top displays resources used on the system, as well as a sorted list of the "top" resource-using processes. Other tools display the state of disk I/O, memory allocation, and network traffic. The authors of these single-purpose tools try to guess what a user would want to see while analyzing a system and to provide that information.

Making running operating systems easier to understand, debug, and tune is an active area of operating system research and implementation. The cycle of enabling tracing as system problems occur and analyzing the traces later is being broken by a new generation of kernel-enabled performance analysis tools. Further, these tools are not single-purpose or merely for sections of code that were written to emit debugging data. The Solaris 10 DTrace dynamic tracing facility is a leading example of such a tool.

2.9.3 DTrace

DTrace is a facility that dynamically adds probes to a running system, both in user processes and in the kernel. These probes can be queried via the D programming language to determine an astonishing amount about the kernel, the system state, and process activities. For example, Figure 2.22 follows an application as it executes a system call (ioctl) and further shows the functional calls within the kernel as they execute to perform the system call. Lines ending with "U" are executed in user mode, and lines ending in "K" in kernel mode.

Debugging the interactions between user-level and kernel code is nearly impossible without a toolset that understands both sets of code and can instrument the interactions. For that toolset to be truly useful, it must be able to debug any area of a system, including areas that were not written with debugging in mind, and do so without affecting system reliability. This tool must also have a minimum performance impact—ideally it should have no impact when not in use and a proportional impact during use. The DTrace tool meets these requirements and provides a dynamic, safe, low-impact debugging environment.

Until the DTrace framework and tools became available with Solaris 10, kernel debugging was usually shrouded in mystery and accomplished via happenstance and archaic code and tools. For example, CPUs have a breakpoint feature that will halt execution and allow a debugger to examine the state of the system. Then execution can continue until the next breakpoint or termination. This method cannot be used in a multiuser operating-system kernel without negatively affecting all of the users on the system. Profiling, which periodically samples the instruction pointer to determine which code is being executed, can show statistical trends but not individual activities. Code can be included in the kernel to emit specific data under specific circumstances, but that code

```
# ./all.d `pgrep xclock` XEventsQueued
dtrace: script './all.d' matched 52377 probes
CPU FUNCTION
  0 -> XEventsQueued                             U
  0    -> _XEventsQueued                         U
  0       -> _X11TransBytesReadable              U
  0       <- _X11TransBytesReadable              U
  0       -> _X11TransSocketBytesReadable        U
  0       <- _X11TransSocketBytesreadable        U
  0       -> ioctl                               U
  0          -> ioctl                            K
  0             -> getf                          K
  0                -> set_active_fd              K
  0                <- set_active_fd              K
  0             <- getf                          K
  0             -> get_udatamodel                K
  0             <- get_udatamodel                K
  ...
  0             -> releasef                      K
  0                -> clear_active_fd            K
  0                <- clear_active_fd            K
  0                -> cv_broadcast               K
  0                <- cv_broadcast               K
  0             <- releasef                      K
  0          <- ioctl                            K
  0       <- ioctl                               U
  0    <- _XEventsQueued                         U
  0 <- XEventsQueued                             U
```

Figure 2.22 Solaris 10 dtrace follows a system call within the kernel.

slows down the kernel and tends not to be included in the part of the kernel
where the specific problem being debugged is occurring.

In contrast, DTrace runs on production systems—systems that are running
important or critical applications—and causes no harm to the system. It
slows activities while enabled, but after execution it resets the system to its
pre-debugging state. It is also a broad and deep tool. It can broadly debug
everything happening in the system (both at the user and kernel levels and
between the user and kernel layers). DTrace can also delve deeply into code,
showing individual CPU instructions or kernel subroutine activities.

DTrace is composed of a compiler, a framework, providers of probes
written within that framework, and consumers of those probes. DTrace
providers create probes. Kernel structures exist to keep track of all probes that
the providers have created. The probes are stored in a hash table data structure
that is hashed by name and indexed according to unique probe identifiers.
When a probe is enabled, a bit of code in the area to be probed is rewritten
to call dtrace_probe(probe identifier) and then continue with the code's
original operation. Different providers create different kinds of probes. For
example, a kernel system-call probe works differently from a user-process
probe, and that is different from an I/O probe.

DTrace features a compiler that generates a byte code that is run in the
kernel. This code is assured to be "safe" by the compiler. For example, no

loops are allowed, and only specific kernel state modifications are allowed when specifically requested. Only users with the DTrace "privileges" (or "root" users) are allowed to use DTrace, as it can retrieve private kernel data (and modify data if requested). The generated code runs in the kernel and enables probes. It also enables consumers in user mode and enables communications between the two.

A DTrace consumer is code that is interested in a probe and its results. A consumer requests that the provider create one or more probes. When a probe fires, it emits data that are managed by the kernel. Within the kernel, actions called **enabling control blocks**, or ECBs, are performed when probes fire. One probe can cause multiple ECBs to execute if more than one consumer is interested in that probe. Each ECB contains a predicate ("if statement") that can filter out that ECB. Otherwise, the list of actions in the ECB is executed. The most usual action is to capture some bit of data, such as a variable's value at that point of the probe execution. By gathering such data, a complete picture of a user or kernel action can be built. Further, probes firing from both user space and the kernel can show how a user-level action caused kernel-level reactions. Such data are invaluable for performance monitoring and code optimization.

Once the probe consumer terminates, its ECBs are removed. If there are no ECBs consuming a probe, the probe is removed. That involves rewriting the code to remove the dtrace_probe call and put back the original code. Thus, before a probe is created and after it is destroyed, the system is exactly the same, as if no probing occurred.

DTrace takes care to assure that probes do not use too much memory or CPU capacity, which could harm the running system. The buffers used to hold the probe results are monitored for exceeding default and maximum limits. CPU time for probe execution is monitored as well. If limits are exceeded, the consumer is terminated, along with the offending probes. Buffers are allocated per CPU to avoid contention and data loss.

An example of D code and its output shows some of its utility. The following program shows the DTrace code to enable scheduler probes and record the amount of CPU time of each process running with user ID 101 while those probes are enabled (that is, while the program runs):

```
sched:::on-cpu
uid == 101
{
    self->ts = timestamp;
}

sched:::off-cpu
self->ts
{
    @time[execname] = sum(timestamp - self->ts);
    self->ts = 0;
}
```

The output of the program, showing the processes and how much time (in nanoseconds) they spend running on the CPUs, is shown in Figure 2.23.

```
# dtrace -s sched.d
dtrace: script 'sched.d' matched 6 probes
^C
      gnome-settings-d              142354
      gnome-vfs-daemon              158243
      dsdm                          189804
      wnck-applet                   200030
      gnome-panel                   277864
      clock-applet                  374916
      mapping-daemon                385475
      xscreensaver                  514177
      metacity                      539281
      Xorg                          2579646
      gnome-terminal                5007269
      mixer_applet2                 7388447
      java                          10769137
```

Figure 2.23   Output of the D code.

Because DTrace is part of the open-source Solaris 10 operating system, it is being added to other operating systems when those systems do not have conflicting license agreements. For example, DTrace has been added to Mac OS X 10.5 and FreeBSD and will likely spread further due to its unique capabilities. Other operating systems, especially the Linux derivatives, are adding kernel-tracing functionality as well. Still other operating systems are beginning to include performance and tracing tools fostered by research at various institutions, including the Paradyn project.

2.10 Operating-System Generation

It is possible to design, code, and implement an operating system specifically for one machine at one site. More commonly, however, operating systems are designed to run on any of a class of machines at a variety of sites with a variety of peripheral configurations. The system must then be configured or generated for each specific computer site, a process sometimes known as **system generation (SYSGEN)**.

The operating system is normally distributed on disk, on CD-ROM or DVD-ROM, or as an "ISO" image, which is a file in the format of a CD-ROM or DVD-ROM. To generate a system, we use a special program. This SYSGEN program reads from a given file, or asks the operator of the system for information concerning the specific configuration of the hardware system, or probes the hardware directly to determine what components are there. The following kinds of information must be determined.

- What CPU is to be used? What options (extended instruction sets, floating-point arithmetic, and so on) are installed? For multiple CPU systems, each CPU may be described.

- How will the boot disk be formatted? How many sections, or "partitions," will it be separated into, and what will go into each partition?

- How much memory is available? Some systems will determine this value themselves by referencing memory location after memory location until an "illegal address" fault is generated. This procedure defines the final legal address and hence the amount of available memory.

- What devices are available? The system will need to know how to address each device (the device number), the device interrupt number, the device's type and model, and any special device characteristics.

- What operating-system options are desired, or what parameter values are to be used? These options or values might include how many buffers of which sizes should be used, what type of CPU-scheduling algorithm is desired, what the maximum number of processes to be supported is, and so on.

Once this information is determined, it can be used in several ways. At one extreme, a system administrator can use it to modify a copy of the source code of the operating system. The operating system then is completely compiled. Data declarations, initializations, and constants, along with conditional compilation, produce an output-object version of the operating system that is tailored to the system described.

At a slightly less tailored level, the system description can lead to the creation of tables and the selection of modules from a precompiled library. These modules are linked together to form the generated operating system. Selection allows the library to contain the device drivers for all supported I/O devices, but only those needed are linked into the operating system. Because the system is not recompiled, system generation is faster, but the resulting system may be overly general.

At the other extreme, it is possible to construct a system that is completely table driven. All the code is always part of the system, and selection occurs at execution time, rather than at compile or link time. System generation involves simply creating the appropriate tables to describe the system.

The major differences among these approaches are the size and generality of the generated system and the ease of modifying it as the hardware configuration changes. Consider the cost of modifying the system to support a newly acquired graphics terminal or another disk drive. Balanced against that cost, of course, is the frequency (or infrequency) of such changes.

2.11   System Boot

After an operating system is generated, it must be made available for use by the hardware. But how does the hardware know where the kernel is or how to load that kernel? The procedure of starting a computer by loading the kernel is known as *booting* the system. On most computer systems, a small piece of code known as the **bootstrap program** or **bootstrap loader** locates the kernel, loads it into main memory, and starts its execution. Some computer systems, such as PCs, use a two-step process in which a simple bootstrap loader fetches a more complex boot program from disk, which in turn loads the kernel.

When a CPU receives a reset event—for instance, when it is powered up or rebooted—the instruction register is loaded with a predefined memory location, and execution starts there. At that location is the initial bootstrap program. This program is in the form of **read-only memory (ROM)**, because the RAM is in an unknown state at system startup. ROM is convenient because it needs no initialization and cannot easily be infected by a computer virus.

The bootstrap program can perform a variety of tasks. Usually, one task is to run diagnostics to determine the state of the machine. If the diagnostics pass, the program can continue with the booting steps. It can also initialize all aspects of the system, from CPU registers to device controllers and the contents of main memory. Sooner or later, it starts the operating system.

Some systems—such as cellular phones, PDAs, and game consoles—store the entire operating system in ROM. Storing the operating system in ROM is suitable for small operating systems, simple supporting hardware, and rugged operation. A problem with this approach is that changing the bootstrap code requires changing the ROM hardware chips. Some systems resolve this problem by using **erasable programmable read-only memory (EPROM)**, which is read-only except when explicitly given a command to become writable. All forms of ROM are also known as **firmware**, since their characteristics fall somewhere between those of hardware and those of software. A problem with firmware in general is that executing code there is slower than executing code in RAM. Some systems store the operating system in firmware and copy it to RAM for fast execution. A final issue with firmware is that it is relatively expensive, so usually only small amounts are available.

For large operating systems (including most general-purpose operating systems like Windows, Mac OS X, and UNIX) or for systems that change frequently, the bootstrap loader is stored in firmware, and the operating system is on disk. In this case, the bootstrap runs diagnostics and has a bit of code that can read a single block at a fixed location (say block zero) from disk into memory and execute the code from that **boot block**. The program stored in the boot block may be sophisticated enough to load the entire operating system into memory and begin its execution. More typically, it is simple code (as it fits in a single disk block) and knows only the address on disk and length of the remainder of the bootstrap program. GRUB is an example of an open-source bootstrap program for Linux systems. All of the disk-bound bootstrap, and the operating system itself, can be easily changed by writing new versions to disk. A disk that has a boot partition (more on that in Section 12.5.1) is called a **boot disk** or **system disk**.

Now that the full bootstrap program has been loaded, it can traverse the file system to find the operating system kernel, load it into memory, and start its execution. It is only at this point that the system is said to be **running**.

2.12 Summary

Operating systems provide a number of services. At the lowest level, system calls allow a running program to make requests from the operating system directly. At a higher level, the command interpreter or shell provides a mechanism for a user to issue a request without writing a program. Commands may come from files during batch-mode execution or directly from a terminal when in an interactive or time-shared mode. System programs are provided to satisfy many common user requests.

The types of requests vary according to level. The system-call level must provide the basic functions, such as process control and file and device manipulation. Higher-level requests, satisfied by the command interpreter or system programs, are translated into a sequence of system calls. System services can be classified into several categories: program control, status requests, and I/O requests. Program errors can be considered implicit requests for service.

Once the system services are defined, the structure of the operating system can be developed. Various tables are needed to record the information that defines the state of the computer system and the status of the system's jobs.

The design of a new operating system is a major task. It is important that the goals of the system be well defined before the design begins. The type of system desired is the foundation for choices among various algorithms and strategies that will be needed.

Since an operating system is large, modularity is important. Designing a system as a sequence of layers or using a microkernel is considered a good technique. The virtual-machine concept takes the layered approach and treats both the kernel of the operating system and the hardware as though they were hardware. Even other operating systems may be loaded on top of this virtual machine.

Throughout the entire operating-system design cycle, we must be careful to separate policy decisions from implementation details (mechanisms). This separation allows maximum flexibility if policy decisions are to be changed later.

Operating systems are now almost always written in a systems-implementation language or in a higher-level language. This feature improves their implementation, maintenance, and portability. To create an operating system for a particular machine configuration, we must perform system generation.

Debugging process and kernel failures can be accomplished through the use of debuggers and other tools that analyze core dumps. Tools such as DTrace analyze production systems to find bottlenecks and understand other system behavior.

For a computer system to begin running, the CPU must initialize and start executing the bootstrap program in firmware. The bootstrap can execute the operating system directly if the operating system is also in the firmware, or it can complete a sequence in which it loads progressively smarter programs from firmware and disk until the operating system itself is loaded into memory and executed.

Practice Exercises

2.1 What is the purpose of system calls?

2.2 What are the five major activities of an operating system with regard to process management?

2.3 What are the three major activities of an operating system with regard to memory management?

2.4   What are the three major activities of an operating system with regard to secondary-storage management?

2.5   What is the purpose of the command interpreter? Why is it usually separate from the kernel?

2.6   What system calls have to be executed by a command interpreter or shell in order to start a new process?

2.7   What is the purpose of system programs?

2.8   What is the main advantage of the layered approach to system design? What are the disadvantages of using the layered approach?

2.9   List five services provided by an operating system, and explain how each creates convenience for users. In which cases would it be impossible for user-level programs to provide these services? Explain your answer.

2.10   Why do some systems store the operating system in firmware, while others store it on disk?

2.11   How could a system be designed to allow a choice of operating systems from which to boot? What would the bootstrap program need to do?

Exercises

2.12   The services and functions provided by an operating system can be divided into two main categories. Briefly describe the two categories and discuss how they differ.

2.13   Describe three general methods for passing parameters to the operating system.

2.14   Describe how you could obtain a statistical profile of the amount of time spent by a program executing different sections of its code. Discuss the importance of obtaining such a statistical profile.

2.15   What are the five major activities of an operating system with regard to file management?

2.16   What are the advantages and disadvantages of using the same system-call interface for manipulating both files and devices?

2.17   Would it be possible for the user to develop a new command interpreter using the system-call interface provided by the operating system?

2.18   What are the two models of interprocess communication? What are the strengths and weaknesses of the two approaches?

2.19   Why is the separation of mechanism and policy desirable?

2.20   It is sometimes difficult to achieve a layered approach if two components of the operating system are dependent on each other. Identify a scenario in which it is unclear how to layer two system components that require tight coupling of their functionalities.

2.21 What is the main advantage of the microkernel approach to system design? How do user programs and system services interact in a microkernel architecture? What are the disadvantages of using the microkernel approach?

2.22 In what ways is the modular kernel approach similar to the layered approach? In what ways does it differ from the layered approach?

2.23 What is the main advantage for an operating-system designer of using a virtual-machine architecture? What is the main advantage for a user?

2.24 Why is a just-in-time compiler useful for executing Java programs?

2.25 What is the relationship between a guest operating system and a host operating system in a system like VMware? What factors need to be considered in choosing the host operating system?

2.26 The experimental Synthesis operating system has an assembler incorporated in the kernel. To optimize system-call performance, the kernel assembles routines within kernel space to minimize the path that the system call must take through the kernel. This approach is the antithesis of the layered approach, in which the path through the kernel is extended to make building the operating system easier. Discuss the pros and cons of the Synthesis approach to kernel design and system-performance optimization.

Programming Problems

2.27 In Section 2.3, we described a program that copies the contents of one file to a destination file. This program works by first prompting the user for the name of the source and destination files. Write this program using either the Win32 or POSIX API. Be sure to include all necessary error checking, including ensuring that the source file exists.

Once you have correctly designed and tested the program, if you used a system that supports it, run the program using a utility that traces system calls. Linux systems provide the `ptrace` utility, and Solaris systems use the `truss` or `dtrace` command. On Mac OS X, the `ktrace` facility provides similar functionality. As Windows systems do not provide such features, you will have to trace through the Win32 version of this program using a debugger.

Programming Projects

2.28 **Adding a system call to the Linux Kernel**.

In this project, you will study the system-call interface provided by the Linux operating system and learn how user programs communicate with the operating system kernel via this interface. Your task is to incorporate a new system call into the kernel, thereby expanding the functionality of the operating system.

Part 1: Getting Started

A user-mode procedure call is performed by passing arguments to the called procedure either on the stack or through registers, saving the current state and the value of the program counter, and jumping to the beginning of the code corresponding to the called procedure. The process continues to have the same privileges as before.

System calls appear as procedure calls to user programs but result in a change in execution context and privileges. In Linux on the Intel 386 architecture, a system call is accomplished by storing the system-call number into the EAX register, storing arguments to the system call in other hardware registers, and executing a trap instruction (which is the INT 0x80 assembly instruction). After the trap is executed, the system-call number is used to index into a table of code pointers to obtain the starting address for the handler code implementing the system call. The process then jumps to this address, and the privileges of the process are switched from user to kernel mode. With the expanded privileges, the process can now execute kernel code, which may include privileged instructions that cannot be executed in user mode. The kernel code can then carry out the requested services, such as interacting with I/O devices, and can perform process management and other activities that cannot be performed in user mode.

The system call numbers for recent versions of the Linux kernel are listed in /usr/src/linux-2.x/include/asm-i386/unistd.h. (For instance, __NR_close corresponds to the system call close(), which is invoked for closing a file descriptor, and is defined as value 6.) The list of pointers to system-call handlers is typically stored in the file /usr/src/linux-2.x/arch/i386/kernel/entry.S under the heading ENTRY(sys_call_table). Notice that sys_close is stored at entry number 6 in the table to be consistent with the system-call number defined in the unistd.h file. (The keyword .long denotes that the entry will occupy the same number of bytes as a data value of type long.)

Part 2: Building a New Kernel

Before adding a system call to the kernel, you must familiarize yourself with the task of building the binary for a kernel from its source code and booting the machine with the newly built kernel. This activity comprises the following tasks, some of which depend on the particular installation of the Linux operating system in use.

- Obtain the kernel source code for the Linux distribution. If the source code package has already been installed on your machine, the corresponding files might be available under /usr/src/linux or /usr/src/linux-2.x (where the suffix corresponds to the kernel version number). If the package has not yet been installed, it can be downloaded from the provider of your Linux distribution or from http://www.kernel.org.

- Learn how to configure, compile, and install the kernel binary. This will vary among the different kernel distributions, but some typical commands for building the kernel (after entering the directory where the kernel source code is stored) include:

- `make xconfig`

- `make dep`

- `make bzImage`

- Add a new entry to the set of bootable kernels supported by the system. The Linux operating system typically uses utilities such as `lilo` and `grub` to maintain a list of bootable kernels from which the user can choose during machine boot-up. If your system supports `lilo`, add an entry to `lilo.conf`, such as:

```
image=/boot/bzImage.mykernel
label=mykernel
root=/dev/hda5
read-only
```

where `/boot/bzImage.mykernel` is the kernel image and `mykernel` is the label associated with the new kernel. This step will allow you to choose the new kernel during the boot-up process. You will then have the option of either booting the new kernel or booting the unmodified kernel if the newly built kernel does not function properly.

Part 3: Extending the Kernel Source

You can now experiment with adding a new file to the set of source files used for compiling the kernel. Typically, the source code is stored in the `/usr/src/linux-2.x/kernel` directory, although that location may differ in your Linux distribution. There are two options for adding the system call. The first is to add the system call to an existing source file in this directory. The second is to create a new file in the source directory and modify `/usr/src/linux-2.x/kernel/Makefile` to include the newly created file in the compilation process. The advantage of the first approach is that when you modify an existing file that is already part of the compilation process, the Makefile need not be modified.

Part 4: Adding a System Call to the Kernel

Now that you are familiar with the various background tasks corresponding to building and booting Linux kernels, you can begin the process of adding a new system call to the Linux kernel. In this project, the system call will have limited functionality; it will simply transition from user mode to kernel mode, print a message that is logged with the kernel messages, and transition back to user mode. We will call this the *helloworld* system call. While it has only limited functionality, it illustrates the system-call mechanism and sheds light on the interaction between user programs and the kernel.

- Create a new file called `helloworld.c` to define your system call. Include the header files `linux/linkage.h` and `linux/kernel.h`. Add the following code to this file:

```
#include <linux/linkage.h>
#include <linux/kernel.h>
asmlinkage int sys_helloworld() {
    printk(KERN_EMERG "hello world!");

    return 1;
}
```

This creates a system call with the name `sys_helloworld()`. If you choose to add this system call to an existing file in the source directory, all that is necessary is to add the `sys_helloworld()` function to the file you choose. In the code, `asmlinkage` is a remnant from the days when Linux used both C++ and C code and is used to indicate that the code is written in C. The `printk()` function is used to print messages to a kernel log file and therefore may be called only from the kernel. The kernel messages specified in the parameter to `printk()` are logged in the file `/var/log/kernel/warnings`. The function prototype for the `printk()` call is defined in `/usr/include/linux/kernel.h`.

- Define a new system call number for `_NR_helloworld` in `/usr/src/linux-2.x/include/asm-i386/unistd.h`. A user program can use this number to identify the newly added system call. Also be sure to increment the value for `_NR_syscalls`, which is stored in the same file. This constant tracks the number of system calls currently defined in the kernel.

- Add an entry `.long sys_helloworld` to the `sys_call_table` defined in the `/usr/src/linux-2.x/arch/i386/kernel/entry.S` file. As discussed earlier, the system-call number is used to index into this table to find the position of the handler code for the invoked system call.

- Add your file `helloworld.c` to the Makefile (if you created a new file for your system call.) Save a copy of your old kernel binary image (in case there are problems with your newly created kernel). You can now build the new kernel, rename it to distinguish it from the unmodified kernel, and add an entry to the loader configuration files (such as `lilo.conf`). After completing these steps, you can boot either the old kernel or the new kernel that contains your system call.

Part 5: Using the System Call from a User Program

When you boot with the new kernel, it will support the newly defined system call; you now simply need to invoke this system call from a user program. Ordinarily, the standard C library supports an interface for system calls defined for the Linux operating system. As your new system call is not linked into the standard C library, however, invoking your system call will require manual intervention.

As noted earlier, a system call is invoked by storing the appropriate value in a hardware register and performing a trap instruction. Unfortunately, these low-level operations cannot be performed using C language statements and instead require assembly instructions. Fortunately, Linux provides macros for instantiating wrapper functions that contain the appropriate assembly instructions. For instance, the following C program uses the _syscall0() macro to invoke the newly defined system call:

```
#include <linux/errno.h>
#include <sys/syscall.h>
#include <linux/unistd.h>

_syscall0(int, helloworld);

main()
{
    helloworld();
}
```

- The _syscall0 macro takes two arguments. The first specifies the type of the value returned by the system call; the second is the name of the system call. The name is used to identify the system-call number that is stored in the hardware register before the trap instruction is executed. If your system call requires arguments, then a different macro (such as _syscall0, where the suffix indicates the number of arguments) could be used to instantiate the assembly code required for performing the system call.

- Compile and execute the program with the newly built kernel. There should be a message "hello world!" in the kernel log file /var/log/kernel/warnings to indicate that the system call has executed.

As a next step, consider expanding the functionality of your system call. How would you pass an integer value or a character string to the system call and have it printed into the kernel log file? What are the implications of passing pointers to data stored in the user program's address space as opposed to simply passing an integer value from the user program to the kernel using hardware registers?

Wiley Plus

Visit Wiley Plus for

- Source code
- Solutions to practice exercises

- Additional programming problems and exercises
- Labs using an operating system simulator

Bibliographical Notes

Dijkstra [1968] advocated the layered approach to operating-system design. Brinch-Hansen [1970] was an early proponent of constructing an operating system as a kernel (or nucleus) on which more complete systems can be built.

System instrumentation and dynamic tracing are described in Tamches and Miller [1999]. DTrace is discussed in Cantrill et al. [2004]. The DTrace source code is available at `http://src.opensolaris.org/source/`. Cheung and Loong [1995] explore issues of operating-system structure from microkernel to extensible systems.

MS-DOS, Version 3.1, is described in Microsoft [1986]. Windows NT and Windows 2000 are described by Solomon [1998] and Solomon and Russinovich [2000]. Windows 2003 and Windows XP internals are described in Russinovich and Solomon [2005]. Hart [2005] covers Windows systems programming in detail. BSD UNIX is described in McKusick et al. [1996]. Bovet and Cesati [2006] thoroughly discuss the Linux kernel. Several UNIX systems—including Mach—are treated in detail in Vahalia [1996]. Mac OS X is presented at `http://www.apple.com/macosx` and in Singh [2007]. Solaris is fully described in McDougall and Mauro [2007].

The first operating system to provide a virtual machine was the CP/67 on an IBM 360/67. The commercially available IBM VM/370 operating system was derived from CP/67. Details regarding Mach, a microkernel-based operating system, can be found in Young et al. [1987]. Kaashoek et al. [1997] present details regarding exokernel operating systems, wherein the architecture separates management issues from protection, thereby giving untrusted software the ability to exercise control over hardware and software resources.

The specifications for the Java language and the Java virtual machine are presented by Gosling et al. [1996] and by Lindholm and Yellin [1999], respectively. The internal workings of the Java virtual machine are fully described by Venners [1998]. Golm et al. [2002] highlight the JX operating system; Back et al. [2000] cover several issues in the design of Java operating systems. More information on Java is available on the Web at `http://www.javasoft.com`. Details about the implementation of VMware can be found in Sugerman et al. [2001]. Information about the Open Virtual Machine Format can be found at `http://www.vmware.com/appliances/learn/ovf.html`.

Bibliography

[Accetta et al. 1986]   M. Accetta, R. Baron, W. Bolosky, D. B. Golub, R. Rashid, A. Tevanian, and M. Young, "Mach: A New Kernel Foundation for UNIX Development", *Proceedings of the Summer USENIX Conference* (1986).

[Adl-Tabatabai et al. 2007]   A.-R. Adl-Tabatabai, C. Kozyrakis, and B. Saha, "Unlocking Concurrency", *Queue*, Volume 4, Number 10 (2007), pages 24–33.

[Agrawal and Abbadi 1991]   D. P. Agrawal and A. E. Abbadi, "An Efficient and Fault-Tolerant Solution of Distributed Mutual Exclusion", *ACM Transactions on Computer Systems*, Volume 9, Number 1 (1991), pages 1–20.

[Agre 2003]   P. E. Agre, "P2P and the Promise of Internet Equality", *Communications of the ACM*, Volume 46, Number 2 (2003), pages 39–42.

[Ahituv et al. 1987]   N. Ahituv, Y. Lapid, and S. Neumann, "Processing Encrypted Data", *Communications of the ACM*, Volume 30, Number 9 (1987), pages 777–780.

[Ahmed 2000]   I. Ahmed, "Cluster Computing: A Glance at Recent Events", *IEEE Concurrency*, Volume 8, Number 1

[Akl 1983]   S. G. Akl, "Digital Signatures: A Tutorial Survey", *Computer*, Volume 16, Number 2 (1983).

[Akyurek and Salem 1993]   S. Akyurek and K. Salem, "Adaptive Block Rearrangement", *Proceedings of the International Conference on Data Engineering* (1993), pages 182–189.

[Alt 1993]   H. Alt, "Removable Media in Solaris", *Proceedings of the Winter USENIX Conference* (1993).

[Anderson 1990]   T. E. Anderson, "The Performance of Spin Lock Alternatives for Shared-Money Multiprocessors", *IEEE Trans. Parallel Distrib. Syst.*, Volume 1, Number 1 (1990), pages 6–16.

[Anderson et al. 1989]   T. E. Anderson, E. D. Lazowska, and H. M. Levy, "The Performance Implications of Thread Management Alternatives for Shared-Memory Multiprocessors", *IEEE Transactions on Computers*, Volume 38, Number 12 (1989), pages 1631–1644.

[Anderson et al. 1991]   T. E. Anderson, B. N. Bershad, E. D. Lazowska, and H. M. Levy, "Scheduler Activations: Effective Kernel Support for the User-Level Management of Parallelism", *Proceedings of the ACM Symposium on Operating Systems Principles* (1991), pages 95–109.

[Anderson et al. 1995]   T. E. Anderson, M. D. Dahlin, J. M. Neefe, D. A. Patterson, D. S. Roselli, and R. Y. Wang, "Serverless Network File Systems", *Proceedings of the ACM Symposium on Operating Systems Principles* (1995).

[Anderson et al. 2000]   D. Anderson, J. Chase, and A. Vahdat, "Interposed Request Routing for Scalable Network Storage", *Proceedings of the Fourth Symposium on Operating Systems Design and Implementation* (2000).

[Apple 1987]   *Apple Technical Introduction to the Macintosh Family*. Addison-Wesley (1987).

[Asthana and Finkelstein 1995]   P. Asthana and B. Finkelstein, "Superdense Optical Storage", *IEEE Spectrum*, Volume 32, Number 8 (1995), pages 25–31.

[Audsley et al. 1991]   N. C. Audsley, A. Burns, M. F. Richardson, and A. J. Wellings, "Hard Real-Time Scheduling: The Deadline Monotonic Approach", *Proceedings of the IEEE Workshop on Real-Time Operating Systems and Software*.

[Axelsson 1999]   S. Axelsson, "The Base-Rate Fallacy and Its Implications for Intrusion Detection", *Proceedings of the ACM Conference on Computer and Communications Security* (1999), pages 1–7.

923

[Babaoglu and Marzullo 1993]   O. Babaoglu and K. Marzullo. "Consistent Global States of Distributed Systems: Fundamental Concepts and Mechanisms", pages 55–96. Addison-Wesley (1993).

[Bach 1987]   M. J. Bach, *The Design of the UNIX Operating System*, Prentice Hall (1987).

[Back et al. 2000]   G. Back, P. Tullman, L. Stoller, W. C. Hsieh, and J. Lepreau, "Techniques for the Design of Java Operating Systems", *2000 USENIX Annual Technical Conference* (2000).

[Baker et al. 1991]   M. G. Baker, J. H. Hartman, M. D. Kupfer, K. W. Shirriff, and J. K. Ousterhout, "Measurements of a Distributed File System", *Proceedings of the ACM Symposium on Operating Systems Principles* (1991).

[Balakrishnan et al. 2003]   H. Balakrishnan, M. F. Kaashoek, D. Karger, R. Morris, and I. Stoica, "Looking up Data in P2P Systems", *Communications of the ACM*, Volume 46, Number 2 (2003).

[Baldwin 2002]   J. Baldwin, "Locking in the Multithreaded FreeBSD Kernel", *USENIX BSD* (2002).

[Barnes 1993]   G. Barnes, "A Method for Implementing Lock-Free Shared Data Structures", *Proceedings of the ACM Symposium on Parallel Algorithms and Architectures* (1993), pages 261–270.

[Barrera 1991]   J. S. Barrera, "A Fast Mach Network IPC Implementation", *Proceedings of the USENIX Mach Symposium* (1991), pages 1–12.

[Basu et al. 1995]   A. Basu, V. Buch, W. Vogels, and T. von Eicken, "U-Net: A User-Level Network Interface for Parallel and Distributed Computing", *Proceedings of the ACM Symposium on Operating Systems Principles* (1995).

[Bays 1977]   C. Bays, "A Comparison of Next-Fit, First-Fit and Best-Fit", *Communications of the ACM*, Volume 20, Number 3 (1977), pages 191–192.

[Belady 1966]   L. A. Belady, "A Study of Replacement Algorithms for a Virtual-Storage Computer", *IBM Systems Journal*, Volume 5, Number 2 (1966), pages 78–101.

[Belady et al. 1969]   L. A. Belady, R. A. Nelson, and G. S. Shedler, "An Anomaly in Space-Time Characteristics of Certain Programs Running in a Paging Machine", *Communications of the ACM*, Volume 12, Number 6 (1969).

[Bellovin 1989]   S. M. Bellovin, "Security Problems in the TCP/IP Protocol Suite", *Computer Communications Review*, Volume 19:2, (1989), pages 32–48.

[Ben-Ari 1990]   M. Ben-Ari, *Principles of Concurrent and Distributed Programming*, Prentice Hall (1990).

[Benjamin 1990]   C. D. Benjamin, "The Role of Optical Storage Technology for NASA", *Proceedings, Storage and Retrieval Systems and Applications* (1990), pages 10–17.

[Bernstein and Goodman 1980]   P. A. Bernstein and N. Goodman, "Time-Stamp-Based Algorithms for Concurrency Control in Distributed Database Systems", *Proceedings of the International Conference on Very Large Databases* (1980), pages 285–300.

[Bernstein et al. 1987]   A. Bernstein, V. Hadzilacos, and N. Goodman, *Concurrency Control and Recovery in Database Systems*, Addison-Wesley (1987).

[Bershad 1993]   B. Bershad, "Practical Considerations for Non-Blocking Concurrent Objects", *IEEE International Conference on Distributed Computing Systems* (1993), pages 264–273.

[Bershad and Pinkerton 1988]   B. N. Bershad and C. B. Pinkerton, "Watchdogs: Extending the Unix File System", *Proceedings of the Winter USENIX Conference* (1988).

[Bershad et al. 1990]   B. N. Bershad, T. E. Anderson, E. D. Lazowska, and H. M. Levy, "Lightweight Remote Procedure Call", *ACM Transactions on Computer Systems*, Volume 8, Number 1 (1990).

[Bershad et al. 1995]   B. N. Bershad, S. Savage, P. Pardyak, E. G. Sirer, M. Fiuczynski, D. Becker, S. Eggers, and C. Chambers, "Extensibility, Safety and Performance in the SPIN Operating System", *Proceedings of the ACM Symposium on Operating Systems Principles* (1995), pages 267–284.

[Beveridge and Wiener 1997]   J. Beveridge and R. Wiener, *Mutlithreading Applications in Win32*, Addison-Wesley.

[Binding 1985]   C. Binding, "Cheap Concurrency in C", *SIGPLAN Notices*, Volume 20, Number 9 (1985).

[Birrell 1989]   A. D. Birrell, "An Introduction to Programming with Threads", Technical report, DEC-SRC (1989).

[Birrell and Nelson 1984]   A. D. Birrell and B. J. Nelson, "Implementing Remote Procedure Calls", *ACM Transactions on Computer Systems*, Volume 2, Number 1 (1984), pages 39–59.

[Blaauw and Brooks 1997]   G. Blaauw and F. Brooks, *Computer Architecture: Concepts and Evolution*, Addison-Wesley (1997).

[Black 1990]   D. L. Black, "Scheduling Support for Concurrency and Parallelism in the Mach Operating System", *IEEE Computer*, Volume 23, Number 5 (1990), pages 35–43.

[Bobrow et al. 1972]   D. G. Bobrow, J. D. Burchfiel, D. L. Murphy, and R. S. Tomlinson, "TENEX, a Paged Time Sharing System for the PDP-10", *Communications of the ACM*, Volume 15, Number 3.

[Bolosky et al. 1997]   W. J. Bolosky, R. P. Fitzgerald, and J. R. Douceur, "Distributed Schedule Management in the Tiger Video Fileserver", *Proceedings of the ACM Symposium on Operating Systems Principles* (1997), pages 212–223.

[Bonwick 1994]   J. Bonwick, "The Slab Allocator: An Object-Caching Kernel Memory Allocator", *USENIX Summer*.

[Bonwick and Adams 2001]   J. Bonwick and J. Adams, "Magazines and Vmem: Extending the Slab Allocator to Many CPUs and Arbitrary Resources", *Proceedings of the 2001 USENIX Annual Technical Conference* (2001).

[Bovet and Cesati 2002]   D. P. Bovet and M. Cesati, *Understanding the Linux Kernel, Second Edition*, O'Reilly & Associates (2002).

[Bovet and Cesati 2006]   D. Bovet and M. Cesati, *Understanding the Linux Kernel, Third Edition*, O'Reilly & Associates (2006).

[Brain 1996]   M. Brain, *Win32 System Services, Second Edition*, Prentice Hall (1996).

[Brent 1989]   R. Brent, "Efficient Implementation of the First-Fit Strategy for Dynamic Storage Allocation", *ACM Transactions on Programming Languages and Systems*, Volume 11, Number 3 (1989).

[Brereton 1986]   O. P. Brereton, "Management of Replicated Files in a UNIX Environment", *Software—Practice and Experience*, Volume 16, (1986), pages 771–780.

[Brinch-Hansen 1970]   P. Brinch-Hansen, "The Nucleus of a Multiprogramming System", *Communications of the ACM*, Volume 13, Number 4 (1970), pages 238–241 and 250.

[Brinch-Hansen 1972]   P. Brinch-Hansen, "Structured Multiprogramming", *Communications of the ACM*, Volume 15, Number 7 (1972), pages 574–578.

[Brinch-Hansen 1973]   P. Brinch-Hansen, *Operating System Principles*, Prentice Hall (1973).

[Brookshear 2003]   J. G. Brookshear, *Computer Science: An Overview, Seventh Edition*, Addison-Wesley.

[Brownbridge et al. 1982]   D. R. Brownbridge, L. F. Marshall, and B. Randell, "The Newcastle Connection or UNIXes of the World Unite!", *Software—Practice and Experience*, Volume 12, Number 12 (1982), pages 1147–1162.

[Burns 1978]   J. E. Burns, "Mutual Exclusion with Linear Waiting Using Binary Shared Variables", *SIGACT News*, Volume 10, Number 2 (1978), pages 42–47.

[Butenhof 1997]   D. Butenhof, *Programming with POSIX Threads*, Addison-Wesley (1997).

[Buyya 1999]   R. Buyya, *High Performance Cluster Computing: Architectures and Systems*, Prentice Hall.

[Callaghan 2000]   B. Callaghan, *NFS Illustrated*, Addison-Wesley (2000).

[Cantrill et al. 2004]   B. M. Cantrill, M. W. Shapiro, and A. H. Leventhal, "Dynamic Instrumation of Production Systems", *2004 USENIX Annual Technical Conference* (2004).

[Carr and Hennessy 1981]   W. R. Carr and J. L. Hennessy, "WSClock—A Simple and Effective Algorithm for Virtual Memory Management", *Proceedings of the ACM Symposium on Operating Systems Principles* (1981).

[Carvalho and Roucairol 1983]   O. S. Carvalho and G. Roucairol, "On Mutual Exclusion in Computer Networks", *Communications of the ACM*, Volume 26, Number 2 (1983), pages 146–147.

[Ceruzzi 1998]   P. E. Ceruzzi, *A History of Modern Computing*, MIT Press (1998).

[Chandy and Lamport 1985]   K. M. Chandy and L. Lamport, "Distributed Snapshots: Determining Global States of Distributed Systems", *ACM Transactions on Computer Systems*, Volume 3, Number 1 (1985), pages 63–75.

[Chang 1980]   E. Chang, "N-Philosophers: An Exercise in Distributed Control", *Computer Networks*, Volume 4, Number 2 (1980), pages 71–76.

[Chang and Mergen 1988]   A. Chang and M. F. Mergen, "801 Storage: Architecture and Programming", *ACM Transactions on Computer Systems*, Volume 6, Number 1 (1988), pages 28–50.

[Chase et al. 1994]   J. S. Chase, H. M. Levy, M. J. Feeley, and E. D. Lazowska, "Sharing and Protection in a Single-Address-Space Operating System", *ACM Transactions on Computer Systems*, Volume 12, Number 4 (1994).

[Chen et al. 1994]   P. M. Chen, E. K. Lee, G. A. Gibson, R. H. Katz, and D. A. Patterson, "RAID: High-Performance, Reliable Secondary Storage", *ACM Computing Surveys*, Volume 26, Number 2 (1994), pages 145–185.

[Cheriton 1988]   D. Cheriton, "The V Distributed System", *Communications of the ACM*, Volume 31, Number 3 (1988), pages 314–333.

[Cheriton et al. 1979]   D. R. Cheriton, M. A. Malcolm, L. S. Melen, and G. R. Sager, "Thoth, a Portable Real-Time Operating System", *Communications of the ACM*, Volume 22, Number 2 (1979).

[Cheswick et al. 2003]   W. Cheswick, S. Bellovin, and A. Rubin, *Firewalls and Internet Security: Repelling the Wily Hacker*, second edition, Addison-Wesley (2003).

[Cheung and Loong 1995]   W. H. Cheung and A. H. S. Loong, "Exploring Issues of Operating Systems Structuring: From Microkernel to Extensible Systems", *Operating Systems Review*, Volume 29, Number 4 (1995), pages 4–16.

[Chi 1982]   C. S. Chi, "Advances in Computer Mass Storage Technology", *Computer*, Volume 15, Number 5 (1982).

[Coffman et al. 1971]   E. G. Coffman, M. J. Elphick, and A. Shoshani, "System Deadlocks", *Computing Surveys*, Volume 3, Number 2 (1971), pages 67–78.

[Cohen and Jefferson 1975]   E. S. Cohen and D. Jefferson, "Protection in the Hydra Operating System", *Proceedings of the ACM Symposium on Operating Systems Principles* (1975), pages 141–160.

[Cohen and Woodring 1997]   A. Cohen and M. Woodring, *Win32 Multithreaded Programming*, O'Reilly & Associates (1997).

[Comer 2000]   D. Comer, *Internetworking with TCP/IP, Volume I, Fourth Edition*, Prentice Hall (2000).

[Corbato and Vyssotsky 1965]   F. J. Corbato and V. A. Vyssotsky, "Introduction and Overview of the MULTICS System", *Proceedings of the AFIPS Fall Joint Computer Conference* (1965), pages 185–196.

[Corbato et al. 1962]   F. J. Corbato, M. Merwin-Daggett, and R. C. Daley, "An Experimental Time-Sharing System", *Proceedings of the AFIPS Fall Joint Computer Conference* (1962), pages 335–344.

[Cormen et al. 2001]   T. H. Cormen, C. E. Leiserson, R. L. Rivest, and C. Stein, *Introduction to Algorithms, Second Edition*, MIT Press (2001).

[Coulouris et al. 2001]   G. Coulouris, J. Dollimore, and T. Kindberg, *Distributed Systems Concepts and Designs, Third Edition*, Addison Wesley (2001).

[Courtois et al. 1971]   P. J. Courtois, F. Heymans, and D. L. Parnas, "Concurrent Control with 'Readers' and 'Writers'", *Communications of the ACM*, Volume 14, Number 10 (1971), pages 667–668.

[Culler et al. 1998]   D. E. Culler, J. P. Singh, and A. Gupta, *Parallel Computer Architecture: A Hardware/Software Approach*, Morgan Kaufmann Publishers Inc. (1998).

[Custer 1994]   H. Custer, *Inside the Windows NT File System*, Microsoft Press (1994).

[Dabek et al. 2001]   F. Dabek, M. F. Kaashoek, D. Karger, R. Morris, and I. Stoica, "Wide-Area Cooperative Storage with CFS", *Proceedings of the ACM Symposium on Operating Systems Principles* (2001), pages 202–215.

[Daley and Dennis 1967]   R. C. Daley and J. B. Dennis, "Virtual Memory, Processes, and Sharing in Multics", *Proceedings of the ACM Symposium on Operating Systems Principles* (1967), pages 121–128.

[Davcev and Burkhard 1985]   D. Davcev and W. A. Burkhard, "Consistency and Recovery Control for Replicated Files", *Proceedings of the ACM Symposium on Operating Systems Principles* (1985).

[Davies 1983]   D. W. Davies, "Applying the RSA Digital Signature to Electronic Mail", *Computer*, Volume 16, Number 2 (1983), pages 55–62.

[deBruijn 1967]   N. G. deBruijn, "Additional Comments on a Problem in Concurrent Programming and Control", *Communications of the ACM*, Volume 10, Number 3 (1967), pages 137–138.

[Deitel 1990]   H. M. Deitel, *An Introduction to Operating Systems, Second Edition*, Addison-Wesley.

[Denning 1968]   P. J. Denning, "The Working Set Model for Program Behavior", *Communications of the ACM*, Volume 11, Number 5 (1968), pages 323–333.

[Denning 1980]   P. J. Denning, "Working Sets Past and Present", *IEEE Transactions on Software Engineering*, Volume SE-6, Number 1 (1980), pages 64–84.

[Denning 1982]   D. E. Denning, *Cryptography and Data Security*, Addison-Wesley (1982).

[Denning 1983]   D. E. Denning, "Protecting Public Keys and Signature Keys", *Computer*, Volume 16, Number 2.

[Denning 1984]   D. E. Denning, "Digital Signatures with RSA and Other Public-Key Cryptosystems", *Communications of the ACM*, Volume 27, Number 4 (1984), pages 388–392.

[Denning and Denning 1979]   D. E. Denning and P. J. Denning, "Data Security", *ACM Computing Surveys*, Volume 11, Number 3 (1979), pages 227–249.

[Dennis 1965]   J. B. Dennis, "Segmentation and the Design of Multiprogrammed Computer Systems", *Communications of the ACM*, Volume 8, Number 4 (1965), pages 589–602.

[Dennis and Horn 1966]   J. B. Dennis and E. C. V. Horn, "Programming Semantics for Multiprogrammed Computations", *Communications of the ACM*, Volume 9, Number 3 (1966).

[Di Pietro and Mancini 2003]   R. Di Pietro and L. V. Mancini, "Security and Privacy Issues of Handheld and Wearable Wireless Devices", *Communications of the ACM*, Volume 46, Number 9 (2003), pages 74–79.

[Diffie and Hellman 1976]   W. Diffie and M. E. Hellman, "New Directions in Cryptography", *IEEE Transactions on Information Theory*, Volume 22, Number 6 (1976), pages 644–654.

[Diffie and Hellman 1979]   W. Diffie and M. E. Hellman, "Privacy and Authentication", *Proceedings of the IEEE*.

[Dijkstra 1965a]   E. W. Dijkstra, "Cooperating Sequential Processes", Technical report, Technological University, Eindhoven, the Netherlands (1965).

[Dijkstra 1965b]   E. W. Dijkstra, "Solution of a Problem in Concurrent Programming Control", *Communications of the ACM*, Volume 8, Number 9 (1965), page 569.

[Dijkstra 1968]   E. W. Dijkstra, "The Structure of the THE Multiprogramming System", *Communications of the ACM*, Volume 11, Number 5 (1968), pages 341–346.

[Dijkstra 1971]   E. W. Dijkstra, "Hierarchical Ordering of Sequential Processes", *Acta Informatica*, Volume 1, Number 2 (1971), pages 115–138.

[DoD 1985]   *Trusted Computer System Evaluation Criteria*. Department of Defense (1985).

[Dougan et al. 1999]   C. Dougan, P. Mackerras, and V. Yodaiken, "Optimizing the Idle Task and Other MMU Tricks", *Proceedings of the Symposium on Operating System Design and Implementation*.

[Douglis and Ousterhout 1991]   F. Douglis and J. K. Ousterhout, "Transparent Process Migration: Design Alternatives and the Sprite Implementation", *Software—Practice and Experience*, Volume 21, Number 8 (1991).

[Douglis et al. 1994]   F. Douglis, F. Kaashoek, K. Li, R. Caceres, B. Marsh, and J. A. Tauber, "Storage Alternatives for Mobile Computers", *Proceedings of the Symposium on Operating Systems Design and Implementation* (1994).

[Douglis et al. 1995]   F. Douglis, P. Krishnan, and B. Bershad, "Adaptive Disk Spin-Down Policies for Mobile Computers", *Proceedings of the USENIX Symposium on Mobile and Location Independent Computing* (1995).

[Draves et al. 1991]   R. P. Draves, B. N. Bershad, R. F. Rashid, and R. W. Dean, "Using Continuations to Implement Thread Management and Communication in Operating Systems", *Proceedings of the ACM Symposium on Operating Systems Principles* (1991), pages 122–136.

[Druschel and Peterson 1993]   P. Druschel and L. L. Peterson, "Fbufs: A High-Bandwidth Cross-Domain Transfer Facility", *Proceedings of the ACM Symposium on Operating Systems Principles*.

[Eastlake 1999]   D. Eastlake, "Domain Name System Security Extensions", *Network Working Group, Request for Comments: 2535* (1999).

[Eisenberg and McGuire 1972]   M. A. Eisenberg and M. R. McGuire, "Further Comments on Dijkstra's Concurrent Programming Control Problem", *Communications of the ACM*, Volume 15, Number 11 (1972), page 999.

[Ekanadham and Bernstein 1979]   K. Ekanadham and A. J. Bernstein, "Conditional Capabilities", *IEEE Transactions on Software Engineering*, Volume SE-5, Number 5 (1979), pages 458–464.

[Engelschall 2000]   R. Engelschall, "Portable Multithreading: The Signal Stack Trick For User-Space Thread Creation", *Proceedings of the 2000 USENIX Annual Technical Conference* (2000).

[Eswaran et al. 1976]   K. P. Eswaran, J. N. Gray, R. A. Lorie, and I. L. Traiger, "The Notions of Consistency and Predicate Locks in a Database System", *Communications of the ACM*, Volume 19, Number 11 (1976), pages 624–633.

[Fang et al. 2001]   Z. Fang, L. Zhang, J. B. Carter, W. C. Hsieh, and S. A. McKee, "Reevaluating Online Superpage Promotion with Hardware Support", *Proceedings of the International Symposium on High-Performance Computer Architecture*, Volume 50, Number 5 (2001).

[Farrow 1986a]   R. Farrow, "Security for Superusers, or How to Break the UNIX System", *UNIX World* (May 1986).

[Farrow 1986b]   R. Farrow, "Security Issues and Strategies for Users", *UNIX World* (April 1986).

[Fidge 1991]   C. Fidge, "Logical Time in Distributed Computing Systems", *Computer*, Volume 24, Number 8 (1991).

[Filipski and Hanko 1986]   A. Filipski and J. Hanko, "Making UNIX Secure", *Byte* (April 1986).

[Fisher 1981]   J. A. Fisher, "Trace Scheduling: A Technique for Global Microcode Compaction", *IEEE Transactions on Computers*, Volume 30, Number 7 (1981), pages 478–490.

[Folk and Zoellick 1987]   M. J. Folk and B. Zoellick, *File Structures*, Addison-Wesley (1987).

[Forrest et al. 1996]   S. Forrest, S. A. Hofmeyr, and T. A. Longstaff, "A Sense of Self for UNIX Processes", *Proceedings of the IEEE Symposium on Security and Privacy* (1996), pages 120–128.

[Fortier 1989]   P. J. Fortier, *Handbook of LAN Technology*, McGraw-Hill (1989).

[Frah 2001]   G. Frah, *The Universal History of Computing*, John Wiley and Sons (2001).

[Frauenfelder 2005]   M. Frauenfelder, *The Computer—An Illustrated History*, Carlton Books (2005).

[Freedman 1983]   D. H. Freedman, "Searching for Denser Disks", *Infosystems* (1983), page 56.

[Freiberger and Swaine 2000]   P. Freiberger and M. Swaine, *Fire in the Valley—The Making of the Personal Computer*, McGraw-Hill (2000).

[Fuhrt 1994]   B. Fuhrt, "Multimedia Systems: An Overview", *IEEE MultiMedia*, Volume 1, Number 1 (1994).

[Fujitani 1984]   L. Fujitani, "Laser Optical Disk: The Coming Revolution in On-Line Storage", *Communications of the ACM*, Volume 27, Number 6 (1984), pages 546–554.

[Gait 1988]   J. Gait, "The Optical File Cabinet: A Random-Access File System for Write-On Optical Disks", *Computer*, Volume 21, Number 6 (1988).

[Ganapathy and Schimmel 1998]   N. Ganapathy and C. Schimmel, "General Purpose Operating System Support for Multiple Page Sizes", *Proceedings of the USENIX Technical Conference* (1998).

[Ganger et al. 2002]   G. R. Ganger, D. R. Engler, M. F. Kaashoek, H. M. Briceno, R. Hunt, and T. Pinckney, "Fast and Flexible Application-Level Networking on Exokernel Systems", *ACM Transactions on Computer Systems*, Volume 20, Number 1 (2002), pages 49–83.

[Garcia-Molina 1982]   H. Garcia-Molina, "Elections in Distributed Computing Systems", *IEEE Transactions on Computers*, Volume C-31, Number 1 (1982).

[Garfinkel et al. 2003]   S. Garfinkel, G. Spafford, and A. Schwartz, *Practical UNIX & Internet Security*, O'Reilly & Associates (2003).

[Ghemawat et al. 2003]   S. Ghemawat, H. Gobioff, and S.-T. Leung, "The Google File System", *Proceedings of the ACM Symposium on Operating Systems Principles* (2003).

[Gibson et al. 1997a]   G. Gibson, D. Nagle, K. Amiri, F. Chang, H. Gobioff, E. Riedel, D. Rochberg, and J. Zelenka, "Filesystems for Network-Attached Secure Disks", Technical report, Carnegie-Mellon University (1997).

[Gibson et al. 1997b]   G. A. Gibson, D. Nagle, K. Amiri, F. W. Chang, E. M. Feinberg, H. Gobioff, C. Lee, B. Ozceri, E. Riedel, D. Rochberg, and J. Zelenka, "File Server Scaling with Network-Attached Secure Disks", *Measurement and Modeling of Computer Systems* (1997), pages 272–284.

[Gifford 1982]   D. K. Gifford, "Cryptographic Sealing for Information Secrecy and Authentication", *Communications of the ACM*, Volume 25, Number 4 (1982), pages 274–286.

[Goetz et al. 2006]   B. Goetz, T. Peirls, J. Bloch, J. Bowbeer, D. Holmes, and D. Lea, *Java Concurrency in Practice*, Addison-Wesley (2006).

[Goldberg et al. 1996]   I. Goldberg, D. Wagner, R. Thomas, and E. A. Brewer, "A Secure Environment for Untrusted Helper Applications", *Proceedings of the 6th Usenix Security Symposium* (1996).

[Golden and Pechura 1986]   D. Golden and M. Pechura, "The Structure of Microcomputer File Systems", *Communications of the ACM*, Volume 29, Number 3 (1986), pages 222–230.

[Golding et al. 1995]   R. A. Golding, P. B. II, C. Staelin, T. Sullivan, and J. Wilkes, "Idleness is Not Sloth", *USENIX Winter* (1995), pages 201–212.

[Golm et al. 2002]   M. Golm, M. Felser, C. Wawersich, and J. Kleinoder, "The JX Operating System", *2002 USENIX Annual Technical Conference* (2002).

[Gong 2002]   L. Gong, "Peer-to-Peer Networks in Action", *IEEE Internet Computing*, Volume 6, Number 1 (2002).

[Gong et al. 1997]   L. Gong, M. Mueller, H. Prafullchandra, and R. Schemers, "Going Beyond the Sandbox: An Overview of the New Security Architecture in the Java Development Kit 1.2", *Proceedings of the USENIX Symposium on Internet Technologies and Systems* (1997).

[Goodman et al. 1989]   J. R. Goodman, M. K. Vernon, and P. J. Woest, "Efficient Synchronization Primitives for Large-Scale Cache-Coherent Multiprocessors", *Proceedings of the International Conference on Architectural Support for Programming Languages and Operating Systems* (1989).

[Gosling et al. 1996]   J. Gosling, B. Joy, and G. Steele, *The Java Language Specification*, Addison-Wesley.

[Govindan and Anderson 1991]   R. Govindan and D. P. Anderson, "Scheduling and IPC Mechanisms for Continuous Media", *Proceedings of the ACM Symposium on Operating Systems Principles* (1991), pages 68–80.

[Grampp and Morris 1984]   F. T. Grampp and R. H. Morris, "UNIX Operating-System Security", *AT&T Bell Laboratories Technical Journal*, Volume 63, Number 8 (1984), pages 1649–1672.

[Gray 1978]   J. N. Gray, "Notes on Data Base Operating Systems", in **[Bayer et al. 1978]** (1978).

[Gray 1981]   J. N. Gray, "The Transaction Concept: Virtues and Limitations", *Proceedings of the International Conference on Very Large Databases* (1981), pages 144–154.

[Gray 1997]   J. Gray, *Interprocess Communications in UNIX*, Prentice Hall (1997).

[Gray et al. 1981]   J. N. Gray, P. R. McJones, and M. Blasgen, "The Recovery Manager of the System R Database Manager", *ACM Computing Surveys*, Volume 13, Number 2 (1981), pages 223–242.

[Greenawalt 1994]   P. Greenawalt, "Modeling Power Management for Hard Disks", *Proceedings of the Symposium on Modeling and Simulation of Computer Telecommunication Systems* (1994), pages 62–66.

[Grosshans 1986]   D. Grosshans, *File Systems Design and Implementation*, Prentice Hall (1986).

[Habermann 1969]   A. N. Habermann, "Prevention of System Deadlocks", *Communications of the ACM*, Volume 12, Number 7 (1969), pages 373–377, 385.

[Hall et al. 1996]   L. Hall, D. Shmoys, and J. Wein, "Scheduling To Minimize Average Completion Time: Off-line and On-line Algorithms", *SODA: ACM-SIAM Symposium on Discrete Algorithms* (1996).

[Hamacher et al. 2002]   C. Hamacher, Z. Vranesic, and S. Zaky, *Computer Organization, Fifth Edition*, McGraw-Hill.

[Han and Ghosh 1998]   K. Han and S. Ghosh, "A Comparative Analysis of Virtual Versus Physical Process-Migration Strategies for Distributed Modeling and Simulation of Mobile Computing Networks", *Wireless Networks*, Volume 4, Number 5 (1998), pages 365–378.

[Harchol-Balter and Downey 1997]   M. Harchol-Balter and A. B. Downey, "Exploiting Process Lifetime Distributions for Dynamic Load Balancing", *ACM Transactions on Computer Systems*, Volume 15, Number 3 (1997).

[Harish and Owens 1999]   V. C. Harish and B. Owens, "Dynamic Load Balancing DNS", *Linux Journal*, Volume 1999, Number 64 (1999).

[Harker et al. 1981]   J. M. Harker, D. W. Brede, R. E. Pattison, G. R. Santana, and L. G. Taft, "A Quarter Century of Disk File Innovation", *IBM Journal of Research and Development*, Volume 25, Number 5 (1981), pages 677–689.

[Harold 2005]   E. R. Harold, *Java Network Programming, Third Edition*, O'Reilly & Associates (2005).

[Harrison et al. 1976]   M. A. Harrison, W. L. Ruzzo, and J. D. Ullman, "Protection in Operating Systems", *Communications of the ACM*, Volume 19, Number 8 (1976), pages 461–471.

[Hart 2005]   J. M. Hart, *Windows System Programming, Third Edition*, Addison-Wesley (2005).

[Hartman and Ousterhout 1995]   J. H. Hartman and J. K. Ousterhout, "The Zebra Striped Network File System", *ACM Transactions on Computer Systems*, Volume 13, Number 3 (1995), pages 274–310.

[Havender 1968]   J. W. Havender, "Avoiding Deadlock in Multitasking Systems", *IBM Systems Journal*, Volume 7, Number 2 (1968), pages 74–84.

[Hecht et al. 1988]   M. S. Hecht, A. Johri, R. Aditham, and T. J. Wei, "Experience Adding C2 Security Features to UNIX", *Proceedings of the Summer USENIX Conference* (1988), pages 133–146.

[Hennessy and Patterson 2002]   J. L. Hennessy and D. A. Patterson, *Computer Architecture: A Quantitative Approach, Third Edition*, Morgan Kaufmann Publishers (2002).

[Hennessy and Patterson 2007]   J. Hennessy and D. Patterson, *Computer Architecture: A Quantitative Approach, Fourth Edition*, Morgan Kaufmann (2007).

[Henry 1984]   G. Henry, "The Fair Share Scheduler", *AT&T Bell Laboratories Technical Journal* (1984).

[Herlihy 1993]   M. Herlihy, "A Methodology for Implementing Highly Concurrent Data Objects", *ACM Transactions on Programming Languages and Systems*, Volume 15, Number 5 (1993).

[Herlihy and Moss 1993]   M. Herlihy and J. E. B. Moss, "Transactional Memory: Architectural Support For Lock-Free Data Structures", *Proceedings of the Twentieth Annual International Symposium on Computer Architecture*.

[Hitz et al. 1995]   D. Hitz, J. Lau, and M. Malcolm, "File System Design for an NFS File Server Appliance", Technical report, NetApp (http://www.netapp.com/tech_library/3002.html) (1995).

[Hoagland 1985]   A. S. Hoagland, "Information Storage Technology—A Look at the Future", *Computer*, Volume 18, Number 7 (1985), pages 60–68.

[Hoare 1972]   C. A. R. Hoare, "Towards a Theory of Parallel Programming", in **[Hoare and Perrott 1972]** (1972).

[Hoare 1974]   C. A. R. Hoare, "Monitors: An Operating System Structuring Concept", *Communications of the ACM*, Volume 17, Number 10 (1974), pages 549–557.

[Holt 1971]   R. C. Holt, "Comments on Prevention of System Deadlocks", *Communications of the ACM*, Volume 14, Number 1 (1971), pages 36–38.

[Holt 1972]   R. C. Holt, "Some Deadlock Properties of Computer Systems", *Computing Surveys*, Volume 4, Number 3 (1972), pages 179–196.

[Holub 2000]   A. Holub, *Taming Java Threads*, Apress (2000).

[Howard et al. 1988]   J. H. Howard, M. L. Kazar, S. G. Menees, D. A. Nichols, M. Satyanarayanan, and R. N. Sidebotham, "Scale and Performance in a Distributed File System", *ACM Transactions on Computer Systems*, Volume 6, Number 1 (1988), pages 55–81.

[Howarth et al. 1961]   D. J. Howarth, R. B. Payne, and F. H. Sumner, "The Manchester University Atlas Operating System, Part II: User's Description", *Computer Journal*, Volume 4, Number 3 (1961).

[Hsiao et al. 1979]   D. K. Hsiao, D. S. Kerr, and S. E. Madnick, *Computer Security*, Academic Press (1979).

[Hu and Perrig 2004]   Y.-C. Hu and A. Perrig, "SPV: A Secure Path Vector Routing Scheme for Securing BGP", *Proceedings of ACM SIGCOMM Conference on Data Communication* (2004).

[Hu et al. 2002]   Y.-C. Hu, A. Perrig, and D. Johnson, "Ariadne: A Secure On-Demand Routing Protocol for Ad Hoc Networks", *Proceedings of the Annual International Conference on Mobile Computing and Networking* (2002).

[Hyman 1985]   D. Hyman, *The Columbus Chicken Statute and More Bonehead Legislation*, S. Greene Press (1985).

[Iacobucci 1988]   E. Iacobucci, *OS/2 Programmer's Guide*, Osborne McGraw-Hill (1988).

[IBM 1983]   *Technical Reference*. IBM Corporation (1983).

[Iliffe and Jodeit 1962]   J. K. Iliffe and J. G. Jodeit, "A Dynamic Storage Allocation System", *Computer Journal*, Volume 5, Number 3 (1962), pages 200–209.

[Iseminger 2000]   D. Iseminger, *Active Directory Services for Microsoft Windows 2000. Technical Reference*, Microsoft Press (2000).

[Jacob and Mudge 1997]   B. Jacob and T. Mudge, "Software-Managed Address Translation", *Proceedings of the International Symposium on High Performance Computer Architecture and Implementation* (1997).

[Jacob and Mudge 1998a]   B. Jacob and T. Mudge, "Virtual Memory in Contemporary Microprocessors", *IEEE Micro Magazine*, Volume 18, (1998), pages 60–75.

[Jacob and Mudge 1998b]   B. Jacob and T. Mudge, "Virtual Memory: Issues of Implementation", *IEEE Computer Magazine*, Volume 31, Number 6 (1998), pages 33–43.

[Jacob and Mudge 2001]   B. Jacob and T. Mudge, "Uniprocessor Virtual Memory Without TLBs", *IEEE Transactions on Computers*, Volume 50, Number 5 (2001).

[Jacobson and Wilkes 1991]   D. M. Jacobson and J. Wilkes, "Disk Scheduling Algorithms Based on Rotational Position", Technical report, Hewlett-Packard Laboratories (1991).

[Jensen et al. 1985]   E. D. Jensen, C. D. Locke, and H. Tokuda, "A Time-Driven Scheduling Model for Real-Time Operating Systems", *Proceedings of the IEEE Real-Time Systems Symposium* (1985).

[Johnstone and Wilson 1998]   M. S. Johnstone and P. R. Wilson, "The Memory Fragmentation Problem: Solved?", *Proceedings of the First International Symposium on Memory Management* (1998).

[Jones and Liskov 1978]   A. K. Jones and B. H. Liskov, "A Language Extension for Expressing Constraints on Data Access", *Communications of the ACM*, Volume 21, Number 5 (1978), pages 358–367.

[Jul et al. 1988]   E. Jul, H. Levy, N. Hutchinson, and A. Black, "Fine-Grained Mobility in the Emerald System", *ACM Transactions on Computer Systems*, Volume 6, Number 1 (1988), pages 109–133.

[Kaashoek et al. 1997]   M. F. Kaashoek, D. R. Engler, G. R. Ganger, H. M. Briceno, R. Hunt, D. Mazieres, T. Pinckney, R. Grimm, J. Jannotti, and K. Mackenzie, "Application Performance and Flexibility on Exokernel Systems", *Proceedings of the ACM Symposium on Operating Systems Principles* (1997), pages 52–65.

[Katz et al. 1989] R. H. Katz, G. A. Gibson, and D. A. Patterson, "Disk System Architectures for High Performance Computing", *Proceedings of the IEEE* (1989).

[Kay and Lauder 1988] J. Kay and P. Lauder, "A Fair Share Scheduler", *Communications of the ACM*, Volume 31, Number 1 (1988), pages 44–55.

[Kenah et al. 1988] L. J. Kenah, R. E. Goldenberg, and S. F. Bate, *VAX/VMS Internals and Data Structures*, Digital Press (1988).

[Kent et al. 2000] S. Kent, C. Lynn, and K. Seo, "Secure Border Gateway Protocol (Secure-BGP)", *IEEE Journal on Selected Areas in Communications*, Volume 18, Number 4 (2000), pages 582–592.

[Kenville 1982] R. F. Kenville, "Optical Disk Data Storage", *Computer*, Volume 15, Number 7 (1982).

[Kessels 1977] J. L. W. Kessels, "An Alternative to Event Queues for Synchronization in Monitors", *Communications of the ACM*, Volume 20, Number 7 (1977), pages 500–503.

[Kieburtz and Silberschatz 1978] R. B. Kieburtz and A. Silberschatz, "Capability Managers", *IEEE Transactions on Software Engineering*, Volume SE-4, Number 6 (1978), pages 467–477.

[Kieburtz and Silberschatz 1983] R. B. Kieburtz and A. Silberschatz, "Access Right Expressions", *ACM Transactions on Programming Languages and Systems*, Volume 5, Number 1 (1983), pages 78–96.

[Kilburn et al. 1961] T. Kilburn, D. J. Howarth, R. B. Payne, and F. H. Sumner, "The Manchester University Atlas Operating System, Part I: Internal Organization", *Computer Journal*, Volume 4, Number 3 (1961), pages 222–225.

[Kim and Spafford 1993] G. H. Kim and E. H. Spafford, "The Design and Implementation of Tripwire: A File System Integrity Checker", Technical report, Purdue University (1993).

[King 1990] R. P. King, "Disk Arm Movement in Anticipation of Future Requests", *ACM Transactions on Computer Systems*, Volume 8, Number 3 (1990), pages 214–229.

[Kistler and Satyanarayanan 1992] J. Kistler and M. Satyanarayanan, "Disconnected Operation in the Coda File System", *ACM Transactions on Computer Systems*, Volume 10, Number 1 (1992).

[Kleinrock 1975] L. Kleinrock, *Queueing Systems, Volume II: Computer Applications*, Wiley-Interscience (1975).

[Knapp 1987] E. Knapp, "Deadlock Detection in Distributed Databases", *Computing Surveys*, Volume 19, Number 4 (1987), pages 303–328.

[Knowlton 1965] K. C. Knowlton, "A Fast Storage Allocator", *Communications of the ACM*, Volume 8, Number 10 (1965), pages 623–624.

[Knuth 1966] D. E. Knuth, "Additional Comments on a Problem in Concurrent Programming Control", *Communications of the ACM*, Volume 9, Number 5 (1966), pages 321–322.

[Knuth 1973] D. E. Knuth, *The Art of Computer Programming, Volume 1: Fundamental Algorithms, Second Edition*, Addison-Wesley (1973).

[Knuth 1998] D. E. Knuth, *The Art of Computer Programming, Volume 3: Sorting and Searching, Second Edition*, Addison-Wesley (1998).

[Koch 1987] P. D. L. Koch, "Disk File Allocation Based on the Buddy System", *ACM Transactions on Computer Systems*, Volume 5, Number 4 (1987), pages 352–370.

[Kongetira et al. 2005] P. Kongetira, K. Aingaran, and K. Olukotun, "Niagara: A 32-Way Multithreaded SPARC Processor", *IEEE Micro Magazine*, Volume 25, Number 2 (2005), pages 21–29.

[Kopetz and Reisinger 1993] H. Kopetz and J. Reisinger, "The Non-Blocking Write Protocol NBW: A Solution to a Real-Time Synchronisation Problem", *IEEE Real-Time Systems Symposium* (1993).

[Kosaraju 1973] S. Kosaraju, "Limitations of Dijkstra's Semaphore Primitives and Petri Nets", *Operating Systems Review*, Volume 7, Number 4 (1973), pages 122–126.

[Kozierok 2005] C. Kozierok, *The TCP/IP Guide*, No Starch Press (2005).

[Kramer 1988] S. M. Kramer, "Retaining SUID Programs in a Secure UNIX", *Proceedings of the Summer USENIX Conference* (1988), pages 107–118.

[Kubiatowicz et al. 2000] J. Kubiatowicz, D. Bindel, Y. Chen, S. Czerwinski, P. Eaton, D. Geels, R. Gummadi, S. Rhea, H. Weatherspoon, W. Weimer, C. Wells, and B. Zhao, "OceanStore: An Architecture for Global-Scale Persistent Storage", *Proc. of Architectural Support for Programming Languages and Operating Systems* (2000).

[Kurose and Ross 2005] J. Kurose and K. Ross, *Computer Networking—A Top-Down Approach Featuring the Internet, Third Edition*, Addison-Wesley (2005).

[Lamport 1974]   L. Lamport, "A New Solution of Dijkstra's Concurrent Programming Problem", *Communications of the ACM*, Volume 17, Number 8 (1974), pages 453–455.

[Lamport 1976]   L. Lamport, "Synchronization of Independent Processes", *Acta Informatica*, Volume 7, Number 1.

[Lamport 1977]   L. Lamport, "Concurrent Reading and Writing", *Communications of the ACM*, Volume 20, Number 11 (1977), pages 806–811.

[Lamport 1978a]   L. Lamport, "The Implementation of Reliable Distributed Multiprocess Systems", *Computer Networks*, Volume 2, Number 2 (1978), pages 95–114.

[Lamport 1978b]   L. Lamport, "Time, Clocks and the Ordering of Events in a Distributed System", *Communications of the ACM*, Volume 21, Number 7 (1978), pages 558–565.

[Lamport 1981]   L. Lamport, "Password Authentication with Insecure Communications", *Communications of the ACM*, Volume 24, Number 11 (1981), pages 770–772.

[Lamport 1986]   L. Lamport, "The Mutual Exclusion Problem", *Communications of the ACM*, Volume 33, Number 2 (1986), pages 313–348.

[Lamport 1987]   L. Lamport, "A Fast Mutual Exclusion Algorithm", *ACM Transactions on Computer Systems*, Volume 5, Number 1 (1987), pages 1–11.

[Lamport 1991]   L. Lamport, "The Mutual Exclusion Problem Has Been Solved", *Communications of the ACM*, Volume 34, Number 1 (1991), page 110.

[Lamport et al. 1982]   L. Lamport, R. Shostak, and M. Pease, "The Byzantine Generals Problem", *ACM Transactions on Programming Languages and Systems*, Volume 4, Number 3 (1982), pages 382–401.

[Lampson 1969]   B. W. Lampson, "Dynamic Protection Structures", *Proceedings of the AFIPS Fall Joint Computer Conference* (1969), pages 27–38.

[Lampson 1971]   B. W. Lampson, "Protection", *Proceedings of the Fifth Annual Princeton Conference on Information Systems Science* (1971), pages 437–443.

[Lampson 1973]   B. W. Lampson, "A Note on the Confinement Problem", *Communications of the ACM*, Volume 10, Number 16 (1973), pages 613–615.

[Lampson and Redell 1979]   B. W. Lampson and D. D. Redell, "Experience with Processes and Monitors in Mesa", *Proceedings of the 7th ACM Symposium on Operating Systems Principles (SOSP)* (1979), pages 43–44.

[Lampson and Sturgis 1976]   B. Lampson and H. Sturgis, "Crash Recovery in a Distributed Data Storage System", Technical report, Xerox Research Center (1976).

[Landwehr 1981]   C. E. Landwehr, "Formal Models of Computer Security", *Computing Surveys*, Volume 13, Number 3 (1981), pages 247–278.

[Lann 1977]   G. L. Lann, "Distributed Systems—Toward a Formal Approach", *Proceedings of the IFIP Congress*.

[Larson and Kajla 1984]   P. Larson and A. Kajla, "File Organization: Implementation of a Method Guaranteeing Retrieval in One Access", *Communications of the ACM*, Volume 27, Number 7 (1984).

[Lauzac et al. 2003]   S. Lauzac, R. Melhem, and D. Mosse, "An Improved Rate-Monotonic Admission Control and Its Applications", *IEEE Transactions on Computers*, Volume 52, Number 3 (2003).

[Lee 2003]   J. Lee, "An End-User Perspective on File-Sharing Systems", *Communications of the ACM*, Volume 46, Number 2 (2003), pages 49–53.

[Lee and Thekkath 1996]   E. K. Lee and C. A. Thekkath, "Petal: Distributed Virtual Disks", *Proceedings of the Seventh International Conference on Architectural Support for Programming Languages and Operating Systems* (1996).

[Leffler et al. 1989]   S. J. Leffler, M. K. McKusick, M. J. Karels, and J. S. Quarterman, *The Design and Implementation of the 4.3BSD UNIX Operating System*, Addison-Wesley (1989).

[Lehmann 1987]   F. Lehmann, "Computer Break-Ins", *Communications of the ACM*, Volume 30, Number 7 (1987).

[Lehoczky et al. 1989]   J. Lehoczky, L. Sha, and Y. Ding, "The Rate Monotonic Scheduling Algorithm: Exact Characterization and Average Case Behaviour", *Proceedings of 10th IEEE Real-Time Systems Symposium* (1989).

[Lempel 1979]   A. Lempel, "Cryptology in Transition", *Computing Surveys*, Volume 11, Number 4 (1979).

[Leslie et al. 1996]   I. M. Leslie, D. McAuley, R. Black, T. Roscoe, P. T. Barham, D. Evers, R. Fairbairns, and E. Hyden, "The Design and Implementation of an Operating System to Support Distributed Multimedia Applications", *IEEE Journal of Selected Areas in Communications*, Volume 14, Number 7 (1996), pages 1280–1297.

[Lett and Konigsford 1968]   A. L. Lett and W. L. Konigsford, "TSS/360: A Time-Shared Operating System", *Proceedings of the AFIPS Fall Joint Computer Conference* (1968), pages 15–28.

[Levin et al. 1975]   R. Levin, E. S. Cohen, W. M. Corwin, F. J. Pollack, and W. A. Wulf, "Policy/Mechanism Separation in Hydra", *Proceedings of the ACM Symposium on Operating Systems Principles* (1975), pages 132–140.

[Levine 2003]   G. Levine, "Defining Deadlock", *Operating Systems Review*, Volume 37, Number 1.

[Levy 1994]   S. Levy, *Hackers*, Penguin Books (1994).

[Lewis and Berg 1998]   B. Lewis and D. Berg, *Multithreaded Programming with Pthreads*, Sun Microsystems Press.

[Lewis and Berg 2000]   B. Lewis and D. Berg, *Multithreaded Programming with Java Technology*, Sun Microsystems Press (2000).

[Lichtenberger and Pirtle 1965]   W. W. Lichtenberger and M. W. Pirtle, "A Facility for Experimentation in Man-Machine Interaction", *Proceedings of the AFIPS Fall Joint Computer Conference* (1965), pages 589–598.

[Lindholm and Yellin 1999]   T. Lindholm and F. Yellin, *The Java Virtual Machine Specification, Second Edition*, Addison-Wesley (1999).

[Ling et al. 2000]   Y. Ling, T. Mullen, and X. Lin, "Analysis of Optimal Thread Pool Size", *Operating System Review*, Volume 34, Number 2 (2000).

[Lipner 1975]   S. Lipner, "A Comment on the Confinement Problem", *Operating System Review*, Volume 9, Number 5 (1975), pages 192–196.

[Lipton 1974]   R. Lipton, *On Synchronization Primitive Systems*. PhD thesis, Carnegie-Mellon University (1974).

[Liskov 1972]   B. H. Liskov, "The Design of the Venus Operating System", *Communications of the ACM*, Volume 15, Number 3 (1972), pages 144–149.

[Liu and Layland 1973]   C. L. Liu and J. W. Layland, "Scheduling Algorithms for Multiprogramming in a Hard Real-Time Environment", *Communications of the ACM*, Volume 20, Number 1 (1973).

[Lobel 1986]   J. Lobel, *Foiling the System Breakers: Computer Security and Access Control*, McGraw-Hill.

[Loo 2003]   A. W. Loo, "The Future of Peer-to-Peer Computing", *Communications of the ACM*, Volume 46, Number 9 (2003), pages 56–61.

[Love 2004]   R. Love, *Linux Kernel Development*, Developer's Library (2004).

[Love 2005]   R. Love, *Linux Kernel Development, Second Edition*, Developer's Library (2005).

[Lowney et al. 1993]   P. G. Lowney, S. M. Freudenberger, T. J. Karzes, W. D. Lichtenstein, R. P. Nix, J. S. O'Donnell, and J. C. Ruttenberg, "The Multiflow Trace Scheduling Compiler", *Journal of Supercomputing*, Volume 7, Number 1-2 (1993), pages 51–142.

[Ludwig 1998]   M. Ludwig, *The Giant Black Book of Computer Viruses, Second Edition*, American Eagle Publications.

[Ludwig 2002]   M. Ludwig, *The Little Black Book of Email Viruses*, American Eagle Publications (2002).

[Lumb et al. 2000]   C. Lumb, J. Schindler, G. R. Ganger, D. F. Nagle, and E. Riedel, "Towards Higher Disk Head Utilization: Extracting Free Bandwidth From Busy Disk Drives", *Symposium on Operating Systems Design and Implementation* (2000).

[Maekawa 1985]   M. Maekawa, "A Square Root Algorithm for Mutual Exclusion in Decentralized Systems", *ACM Transactions on Computer Systems*, Volume 3, Number 2 (1985), pages 145–159.

[Maher et al. 1994]   C. Maher, J. S. Goldick, C. Kerby, and B. Zumach, "The Integration of Distributed File Systems and Mass Storage Systems", *Proceedings of the IEEE Symposium on Mass Storage Systems* (1994), pages 27–31.

[Marsh et al. 1991]   B. D. Marsh, M. L. Scott, T. J. LeBlanc, and E. P. Markatos, "First-Class User-Level Threads", *Proceedings of the 13th ACM Symposium on Operating Systems Principle* (1991), pages 110–121.

[Mattern 1988]   F. Mattern, "Virtual Time and Global States of Distributed Systems", *Workshop on Parallel and Distributed Algorithms* (1988).

[Mattson et al. 1970]   R. L. Mattson, J. Gecsei, D. R. Slutz, and I. L. Traiger, "Evaluation Techniques for Storage Hierarchies", *IBM Systems Journal*, Volume 9, Number 2 (1970), pages 78–117.

[Mauro and McDougall 2007]   J. Mauro and R. McDougall, *Solaris Internals: Core Kernel Architecture*, Prentice Hall.

[McCanne and Jacobson 1993]   S. McCanne and V. Jacobson, "The BSD Packet Filter: A New Architecture for User-level Packet Capture", *USENIX Winter* (1993), pages 259–270.

[McDougall and Laudon 2006]   R. McDougall and J. Laudon, "Multi-Core Processors are Here", *USENIX ;login: The USENIX Magazine*, Volume 31, Number 5 (2006), pages 32–39.

[McDougall and Mauro 2007]   R. McDougall and J. Mauro, *Solaris Internals, Second Edition*, Prentice Hall (2007).

[McGraw and Andrews 1979]   J. R. McGraw and G. R. Andrews, "Access Control in Parallel Programs", *IEEE Transactions on Software Engineering*, Volume SE-5, Number 1 (1979), pages 1–9.

[McKeag and Wilson 1976]   R. M. McKeag and R. Wilson, *Studies in Operating Systems*, Academic Press (1976).

[McKeon 1985]   B. McKeon, "An Algorithm for Disk Caching with Limited Memory", *Byte*, Volume 10, Number 9 (1985), pages 129–138.

[McKusick and Neville-Neil 2005]   M. K. McKusick and G. V. Neville-Neil, *The Design and Implementation of the FreeBSD UNIX Operating System*, Addison Wesley (2005).

[McKusick et al. 1984]   M. K. McKusick, W. N. Joy, S. J. Leffler, and R. S. Fabry, "A Fast File System for UNIX", *ACM Transactions on Computer Systems*, Volume 2, Number 3 (1984), pages 181–197.

[McKusick et al. 1996]   M. K. McKusick, K. Bostic, and M. J. Karels, *The Design and Implementation of the 4.4 BSD UNIX Operating System*, John Wiley and Sons (1996).

[McNairy and Bhatia 2005]   C. McNairy and R. Bhatia, "Montecito: A Dual-Core, Dual-Threaded Itanium Processor", *IEEE Micro Magazine*, Volume 25, Number 2 (2005), pages 10–20.

[McVoy and Kleiman 1991]   L. W. McVoy and S. R. Kleiman, "Extent-like Performance from a UNIX File System", *Proceedings of the Winter USENIX Conference* (1991), pages 33–44.

[Mealy et al. 1966]   G. H. Mealy, B. I. Witt, and W. A. Clark, "The Functional Structure of OS/360", *IBM Systems Journal*, Volume 5, Number 1 (1966).

[Mellor-Crummey and Scott 1991]   J. M. Mellor-Crummey and M. L. Scott, "Algorithms for Scalable Synchronization on Shared-Memory Multiprocessors", *ACM Transactions on Computer Systems*, Volume 9, Number 1 (1991).

[Menasce and Muntz 1979]   D. Menasce and R. R. Muntz, "Locking and Deadlock Detection in Distributed Data Bases", *IEEE Transactions on Software Engineering*, Volume SE-5, Number 3 (1979), pages 195–202.

[Mercer et al. 1994]   C. W. Mercer, S. Savage, and H. Tokuda, "Processor Capacity Reserves: Operating System Support for Multimedia Applications", *International Conference on Multimedia Computing and Systems* (1994).

[Meyer and Seawright 1970]   R. A. Meyer and L. H. Seawright, "A Virtual Machine Time-Sharing System", *IBM Systems Journal*, Volume 9, Number 3 (1970), pages 199–218.

[Microsoft 1986]   *Microsoft MS-DOS User's Reference and Microsoft MS-DOS Programmer's Reference*. Microsoft Press.

[Microsoft 1996]   *Microsoft Windows NT Workstation Resource Kit*. Microsoft Press (1996).

[Microsoft 2000a]   *Microsoft Developer Network Development Library*. Microsoft Press (2000).

[Microsoft 2000b]   *Microsoft Windows 2000 Server Resource Kit*. Microsoft Press (2000).

[Milenkovic 1987]   M. Milenkovic, *Operating Systems: Concepts and Design*, McGraw-Hill (1987).

[Miller and Katz 1993]   E. L. Miller and R. H. Katz, "An Analysis of File Migration in a UNIX Supercomputing Environment", *Proceedings of the Winter USENIX Conference* (1993), pages 421–434.

[Milojicic et al. 2000]   D. S. Milojicic, F. Douglis, Y. Paindaveine, R. Wheeler, and S. Zhou, "Process Migration", *ACM Computing Surveys*, Volume 32, Number 3 (2000), pages 241–299.

[Mockapetris 1987]   P. Mockapetris, "Domain Names—Concepts and Facilities", *Network Working Group, Request for Comments: 1034* (1987).

[Mohan and Lindsay 1983]   C. Mohan and B. Lindsay, "Efficient Commit Protocols for the Tree of Processes Model of Distributed Transactions", *Proceedings of the ACM Symposium on Principles of Database Systems* (1983).

[Mok 1983]   A. K. Mok, *Fundamental Design Problems of Distributed Systems for the Hard Real-Time Environment*. PhD thesis, Massachusetts Institute of Technology, MA (1983).

[Morris 1973]   J. H. Morris, "Protection in Programming Languages", *Communications of the ACM*, Volume 16, Number 1 (1973), pages 15–21.

[Morris and Thompson 1979]   R. Morris and K. Thompson, "Password Security: A Case History", *Communications of the ACM*, Volume 22, Number 11 (1979), pages 594–597.

[Morris et al. 1986]   J. H. Morris, M. Satyanarayanan, M. H. Conner, J. H. Howard, D. S. H. Rosenthal, and F. D. Smith, "Andrew: A Distributed Personal Computing Environment", *Communications of the ACM*, Volume 29, Number 3 (1986), pages 184–201.

[Morshedian 1986]   D. Morshedian, "How to Fight Password Pirates", *Computer*, Volume 19, Number 1 (1986).

[Motorola 1993]   *PowerPC 601 RISC Microprocessor User's Manual.* Motorola Inc. (1993).

[Mullender 1993]   S. Mullender, *Distributed Systems, Third Edition*, Addison-Wesley (1993).

[Myers and Beigl 2003]   B. Myers and M. Beigl, "Handheld Computing", *Computer*, Volume 36, Number 9 (2003).

[Navarro et al. 2002]   J. Navarro, S. Lyer, P. Druschel, and A. Cox, "Practical, Transparent Operating System Support for Superpages", *Proceedings of the USENIX Symposium on Operating Systems Design and Implementation*.

[Needham and Walker 1977]   R. M. Needham and R. D. H. Walker, "The Cambridge CAP Computer and Its Protection System", *Proceedings of the Sixth Symposium on Operating System Principles* (1977).

[Nelson et al. 1988]   M. Nelson, B. Welch, and J. K. Ousterhout, "Caching in the Sprite Network File System", *ACM Transactions on Computer Systems*, Volume 6, Number 1 (1988), pages 134–154.

[Norton and Wilton 1988]   P. Norton and R. Wilton, *The New Peter Norton Programmer's Guide to the IBM PC & PS/2*, Microsoft Press (1988).

[Nutt 2004]   G. Nutt, *Operating Systems: A Modern Perspective, Third Edition*, Addison-Wesley (2004).

[Oaks and Wong 1999]   S. Oaks and H. Wong, *Java Threads, Second Edition*, O'Reilly & Associates.

[Obermarck 1982]   R. Obermarck, "Distributed Deadlock Detection Algorithm", *ACM Transactions on Database Systems*, Volume 7, Number 2 (1982), pages 187–208.

[O'Leary and Kitts 1985]   B. T. O'Leary and D. L. Kitts, "Optical Device for a Mass Storage System", *Computer*, Volume 18, Number 7 (1985).

[Olsen and Kenley 1989]   R. P. Olsen and G. Kenley, "Virtual Optical Disks Solve the On-Line Storage Crunch", *Computer Design*, Volume 28, Number 1 (1989), pages 93–96.

[Organick 1972]   E. I. Organick, *The Multics System: An Examination of Its Structure*, MIT Press (1972).

[Ortiz 2001]   S. Ortiz, "Embedded OSs Gain the Inside Track", *Computer*, Volume 34, Number 11.

[Ousterhout 1991]   J. Ousterhout. "The Role of Distributed State". In CMU Computer Science: a 25th Anniversary Commemorative (1991), R. F. Rashid, Ed., Addison-Wesley (1991).

[Ousterhout et al. 1985]   J. K. Ousterhout, H. D. Costa, D. Harrison, J. A. Kunze, M. Kupfer, and J. G. Thompson, "A Trace-Driven Analysis of the UNIX 4.2 BSD File System", *Proceedings of the ACM Symposium on Operating Systems Principles* (1985), pages 15–24.

[Ousterhout et al. 1988]   J. K. Ousterhout, A. R. Cherenson, F. Douglis, M. N. Nelson, and B. B. Welch, "The Sprite Network-Operating System", *Computer*, Volume 21, Number 2 (1988).

[Parameswaran et al. 2001]   M. Parameswaran, A. Susarla, and A. B. Whinston, "P2P Networking: An Information-Sharing Alternative", *Computer*, Volume 34, Number 7 (2001).

[Parmelee et al. 1972]   R. P. Parmelee, T. I. Peterson, C. C. Tillman, and D. Hatfield, "Virtual Storage and Virtual Machine Concepts", *IBM Systems Journal*, Volume 11, Number 2 (1972), pages 99–130.

[Parnas 1975]   D. L. Parnas, "On a Solution to the Cigarette Smokers' Problem Without Conditional Statements", *Communications of the ACM*, Volume 18, Number 3 (1975), pages 181–183.

[Patil 1971]   S. Patil, "Limitations and Capabilities of Dijkstra's Semaphore Primitives for Coordination Among Processes", Technical report, Massachusetts Institute of Technology (1971).

[Patterson et al. 1988]   D. A. Patterson, G. Gibson, and R. H. Katz, "A Case for Redundant Arrays of Inexpensive Disks (RAID)", *Proceedings of the ACM SIGMOD International Conference on the Management of Data* (1988).

[Pease et al. 1980]   M. Pease, R. Shostak, and L. Lamport, "Reaching Agreement in the Presence of Faults", *Communications of the ACM*, Volume 27, Number 2 (1980), pages 228–234.

[Pechura and Schoeffler 1983]   M. A. Pechura and J. D. Schoeffler, "Estimating File Access Time of Floppy Disks", *Communications of the ACM*, Volume 26, Number 10 (1983), pages 754–763.

[Perlman 1988]   R. Perlman, *Network Layer Protocols with Byzantine Robustness.* PhD thesis, Massachusetts Institute of Technology (1988).

[Peterson 1981]   G. L. Peterson, "Myths About the Mutual Exclusion Problem", *Information Processing Letters*, Volume 12, Number 3 (1981).

[Peterson and Norman 1977]   J. L. Peterson and T. A. Norman, "Buddy Systems", *Communications of the ACM*, Volume 20, Number 6 (1977), pages 421–431.

[Pfleeger and Pfleeger 2003]   C. Pfleeger and S. Pfleeger, *Security in Computing, Third Edition*, Prentice Hall (2003).

[Philbin et al. 1996]   J. Philbin, J. Edler, O. J. Anshus, C. C. Douglas, and K. Li, "Thread Scheduling for Cache Locality", *Architectural Support for Programming Languages and Operating Systems* (1996).

[Pinilla and Gill 2003]   R. Pinilla and M. Gill, "JVM: Platform Independent vs. Performance Dependent", *Operating System Review* (2003).

[Popek 1974]   G. J. Popek, "Protection Structures", *Computer*, Volume 7, Number 6 (1974).

[Popek and Walker 1985]   G. Popek and B. Walker, editors, *The LOCUS Distributed System Architecture*, MIT Press.

[Prieve and Fabry 1976]   B. G. Prieve and R. S. Fabry, "VMIN—An Optimal Variable Space Page-Replacement Algorithm", *Communications of the ACM*, Volume 19, Number 5 (1976), pages 295–297.

[Psaltis and Mok 1995]   D. Psaltis and F. Mok, "Holographic Memories", *Scientific American*, Volume 273, Number 5 (1995), pages 70–76.

[Purdin et al. 1987]   T. D. M. Purdin, R. D. Schlichting, and G. R. Andrews, "A File Replication Facility for Berkeley UNIX", *Software—Practice and Experience*, Volume 17, (1987), pages 923–940.

[Purdom, Jr. and Stigler 1970]   P. W. Purdom, Jr. and S. M. Stigler, "Statistical Properties of the Buddy System", *J. ACM*, Volume 17, Number 4 (1970), pages 683–697.

[Quinlan 1991]   S. Quinlan, "A Cached WORM", *Software—Practice and Experience*, Volume 21, Number 12 (1991).

[Rago 1993]   S. Rago, *UNIX System V Network Programming*, Addison-Wesley (1993).

[Rashid 1986]   R. F. Rashid, "From RIG to Accent to Mach: The Evolution of a Network Operating System", *Proceedings of the ACM/IEEE Computer Society, Fall Joint Computer Conference* (1986).

[Rashid and Robertson 1981]   R. Rashid and G. Robertson, "Accent: A Communication-Oriented Network Operating System Kernel", *Proceedings of the ACM Symposium on Operating System Principles*.

[Raymond 1999]   E. S. Raymond, *The Cathedral & the Bazaar*, O'Reilly & Associates (1999).

[Raynal 1986]   M. Raynal, *Algorithms for Mutual Exclusion*, MIT Press (1986).

[Raynal 1991]   M. Raynal, "A Simple Taxonomy for Distributed Mutual Exclusion Algorithms", *Operating Systems Review*, Volume 25, Number 1 (1991), pages 47–50.

[Raynal and Singhal 1996]   M. Raynal and M. Singhal, "Logical Time: Capturing Causality in Distributed Systems", *Computer*, Volume 29, Number 2 (1996), pages 49–56.

[Reddy and Wyllie 1994]   A. L. N. Reddy and J. C. Wyllie, "I/O issues in a Multimedia System", *Computer*, Volume 27, Number 3 (1994), pages 69–74.

[Redell and Fabry 1974]   D. D. Redell and R. S. Fabry, "Selective Revocation of Capabilities", *Proceedings of the IRIA International Workshop on Protection in Operating Systems* (1974), pages 197–210.

[Redell et al. 1980]   D. D. Redell, Y. K. Dalal, T. R. Horsley, H. C. Lauer, W. C. Lynch, P. R. McJones, H. G. Murray, and S. P. Purcell, "Pilot: An Operating System for a Personal Computer", *Communications of the ACM*, Volume 23, Number 2 (1980), pages 81–92.

[Reed 1983]   D. P. Reed, "Implementing Atomic Actions on Decentralized Data", *ACM Transactions on Computer Systems*, Volume 1, Number 1 (1983), pages 3–23.

[Reed and Kanodia 1979]   D. P. Reed and R. K. Kanodia, "Synchronization with Eventcounts and Sequences", *Communications of the ACM*, Volume 22, Number 2 (1979), pages 115–123.

[Regehr et al. 2000]   J. Regehr, M. B. Jones, and J. A. Stankovic, "Operating System Support for Multimedia: The Programming Model Matters", Technical report, Microsoft Research (2000).

[Reid 1987]   B. Reid, "Reflections on Some Recent Widespread Computer Break-Ins", *Communications of the ACM*, Volume 30, Number 2 (1987), pages 103–105.

[Ricart and Agrawala 1981]   G. Ricart and A. K. Agrawala, "An Optimal Algorithm for Mutual Exclusion in Computer Networks", *Communications of the ACM*, Volume 24, Number 1 (1981).

[Richards 1990]   A. E. Richards, "A File System Approach for Integrating Removable Media Devices and Jukeboxes", *Optical Information Systems*, Volume 10, Number 5 (1990), pages 270–274.

[Richter 1997]   J. Richter, *Advanced Windows*, Microsoft Press (1997).

[Riedel et al. 1998]   E. Riedel, G. A. Gibson, and C. Faloutsos, "Active Storage for Large-Scale Data Mining and Multimedia", *Proceedings of 24th International Conference on Very Large Data Bases* (1998).

[Ripeanu et al. 2002]   M. Ripeanu, A. Immnitchi, and I. Foster, "Mapping the Gnutella Network", *IEEE Internet Computing*, Volume 6, Number 1 (2002).

[Rivest et al. 1978]   R. L. Rivest, A. Shamir, and L. Adleman, "On Digital Signatures and Public Key Cryptosystems", *Communications of the ACM*, Volume 21, Number 2 (1978), pages 120–126.

[Robbins and Robbins 2003]   K. Robbins and S. Robbins, *Unix Systems Programming: Communication, Concurrency and Threads, Second Edition*, Prentice Hall (2003).

[Roberson 2003]   J. Roberson, "ULE: A Modern Scheduler For FreeBSD", *Proceedings of the USENIX BSDCon Conference* (2003).

[Rodeheffer and Schroeder 1991]   T. L. Rodeheffer and M. D. Schroeder, "Automatic Reconfiguration in Autonet", *Proceedings of the ACM Symposium on Operating Systems Principles* (1991).

[Rojas and Hashagen 2000]   R. Rojas and U. Hashagen, *The First Computers—History and Architectures*, MIT Press.

[Rosenblum and Ousterhout 1991]   M. Rosenblum and J. K. Ousterhout, "The Design and Implementation of a Log-Structured File System", *Proceedings of the ACM Symposium on Operating Systems Principles* (1991), pages 1–15.

[Rosenkrantz et al. 1978]   D. J. Rosenkrantz, R. E. Stearns, and P. M. Lewis, "System Level Concurrency Control for Distributed Database Systems", *ACM Transactions on Database Systems*, Volume 3, Number 2 (1978).

[Ruemmler and Wilkes 1991]   C. Ruemmler and J. Wilkes, "Disk Shuffling", Technical report (1991).

[Ruemmler and Wilkes 1993]   C. Ruemmler and J. Wilkes, "Unix Disk Access Patterns", *Proceedings of the Winter USENIX Conference* (1993), pages 405–420.

[Ruemmler and Wilkes 1994]   C. Ruemmler and J. Wilkes, "An Introduction to Disk Drive Modeling", *Computer*, Volume 27, Number 3 (1994), pages 17–29.

[Rushby 1981]   J. M. Rushby, "Design and Verification of Secure Systems", *Proceedings of the ACM Symposium on Operating Systems Principles* (1981), pages 12–21.

[Rushby and Randell 1983]   J. Rushby and B. Randell, "A Distributed Secure System", *Computer*, Volume 16, Number 7 (1983), pages 55–67.

[Russell and Gangemi 1991]   D. Russell and G. T. Gangemi, *Computer Security Basics*, O'Reilly & Associates (1991).

[Russinovich and Solomon 2005]   M. E. Russinovich and D. A. Solomon, *Microsoft Windows Internals, Fourth Edition*, Microsoft Press (2005).

[Saltzer and Schroeder 1975]   J. H. Saltzer and M. D. Schroeder, "The Protection of Information in Computer Systems", *Proceedings of the IEEE* (1975), pages 1278–1308.

[Sandberg 1987]   R. Sandberg, *The Sun Network File System: Design, Implementation and Experience*, Sun Microsystems (1987).

[Sandberg et al. 1985]   R. Sandberg, D. Goldberg, S. Kleiman, D. Walsh, and B. Lyon, "Design and Implementation of the Sun Network Filesystem", *Proceedings of the Summer USENIX Conference* (1985), pages 119–130.

[Sargent and Shoemaker 1995]   M. Sargent and R. Shoemaker, *The Personal Computer from the Inside Out, Third Edition*, Addison-Wesley (1995).

[Sarisky 1983]   L. Sarisky, "Will Removable Hard Disks Replace the Floppy?", *Byte* (1983).

[Satyanarayanan 1990]   M. Satyanarayanan, "Scalable, Secure and Highly Available Distributed File Access", *Computer*, Volume 23, Number 5 (1990), pages 9–21.

[Savage et al. 2000]   S. Savage, D. Wetherall, A. R. Karlin, and T. Anderson, "Practical Network Support for IP Traceback", *Proceedings of ACM SIGCOMM Conference on Data Communication* (2000), pages 295–306.

[Schell 1983]   R. R. Schell, "A Security Kernel for a Multiprocessor Microcomputer", *Computer* (1983).

[Schindler and Gregory 1999]   J. Schindler and G. Gregory, "Automated Disk Drive Characterization", Technical report (1999).

[**Schlichting and Schneider 1982**] R. D. Schlichting and F. B. Schneider, "Understanding and Using Asynchronous Message Passing Primitives", *Proceedings of the Symposium on Principles of Distributed Computing* (1982).

[**Schneider 1982**] F. B. Schneider, "Synchronization in Distributed Programs", *ACM Transactions on Programming Languages and Systems*, Volume 4, Number 2 (1982), pages 125–148.

[**Schneier 1996**] B. Schneier, *Applied Cryptography, Second Edition*, John Wiley and Sons (1996).

[**Schrage 1967**] L. E. Schrage, "The Queue M/G/I with Feedback to Lower Priority Queues", *Management Science*, Volume 13, (1967), pages 466–474.

[**Schwarz and Mattern 1994**] R. Schwarz and F. Mattern, "Detecting Causal Relationships in Distributed Computations: In Search of the Holy Grail", *Distributed Computing*, Volume 7, Number 3 (1994), pages 149–174.

[**Seely 1989**] D. Seely, "Password Cracking: A Game of Wits", *Communications of the ACM*, Volume 32, Number 6.

[**Seltzer et al. 1990**] M. Seltzer, P. Chen, and J. Ousterhout, "Disk Scheduling Revisited", *Proceedings of the Winter USENIX Conference* (1990), pages 313–323.

[**Seltzer et al. 1993**] M. I. Seltzer, K. Bostic, M. K. McKusick, and C. Staelin, "An Implementation of a Log-Structured File System for UNIX", *USENIX Winter* (1993), pages 307–326.

[**Seltzer et al. 1995**] M. I. Seltzer, K. A. Smith, H. Balakrishnan, J. Chang, S. McMains, and V. N. Padmanabhan, "File System Logging Versus Clustering: A Performance Comparison", *USENIX Winter* (1995), pages 249–264.

[**Shrivastava and Panzieri 1982**] S. K. Shrivastava and F. Panzieri, "The Design of a Reliable Remote Procedure Call Mechanism", *IEEE Transactions on Computers*, Volume C-31, Number 7 (1982).

[**Siddha et al. 2007**] S. Siddha, V. Pallipadi, and A. Mallick, "Process Scheduling Challenges in the Era of Multi-Core Processors", *Intel Technology Journal*, Volume 11, (2007).

[**Silberschatz et al. 2001**] A. Silberschatz, H. F. Korth, and S. Sudarshan, *Database System Concepts, Fourth Edition*, McGraw-Hill (2001).

[**Silverman 1983**] J. M. Silverman, "Reflections on the Verification of the Security of an Operating System Kernel", *Proceedings of the ACM Symposium on Operating Systems Principles* (1983).

[**Silvers 2000**] C. Silvers, "UBC: An Efficient Unified I/O and Memory Caching Subsystem for NetBSD", *USENIX Annual Technical Conference—FREENIX Track* (2000).

[**Simmons 1979**] G. J. Simmons, "Symmetric and Asymmetric Encryption", *Computing Surveys*, Volume 11, Number 4 (1979), pages 304–330.

[**Sincerbox 1994**] G. T. Sincerbox, editor, *Selected Papers on Holographic Storage*, Optical Engineering Press (1994).

[**Singh 2007**] A. Singh, *Mac OS X Internals : A Systems Approach*, Addison-Wesley (2007).

[**Singhal 1989**] M. Singhal, "Deadlock Detection in Distributed Systems", *Computer*, Volume 22, Number 11 (1989).

[**Sirer et al. 1999**] E. G. Sirer, R. Grimm, A. J. Gregory, and B. N. Bershad, "Design and Implementation of a Distributed Virtual Machine for Networked Computers", *Symposium on Operating Systems Principles* (1999).

[**Smith 1982**] A. J. Smith, "Cache Memories", *ACM Computing Surveys*, Volume 14, Number 3 (1982).

[**Smith 1985**] A. J. Smith, "Disk Cache-Miss Ratio Analysis and Design Considerations", *ACM Transactions on Computer Systems*, Volume 3, Number 3 (1985), pages 161–203.

[**Sobti et al. 2004**] S. Sobti, N. Garg, F. Zheng, J. Lai, Y. Shao, C. Zhang, E. Ziskind, A. Krishnamurthy, and R. Wang, "Segank: A Distributed Mobile Storage System", *Proceedings of the Third USENIX Conference on File and Storage Technologies* (2004).

[**Solomon 1998**] D. A. Solomon, *Inside Windows NT, Second Edition*, Microsoft Press (1998).

[**Solomon and Russinovich 2000**] D. A. Solomon and M. E. Russinovich, *Inside Microsoft Windows 2000, Third Edition*, Microsoft Press (2000).

[**Spafford 1989**] E. H. Spafford, "The Internet Worm: Crisis and Aftermath", *Communications of the ACM*, Volume 32, Number 6 (1989), pages 678–687.

[**Spector and Schwarz 1983**] A. Z. Spector and P. M. Schwarz, "Transactions: A Construct for Reliable Distributed Computing", *ACM SIGOPS Operating Systems Review*, Volume 17, Number 2 (1983), pages 18–35.

[**Stallings 2000a**] W. Stallings, *Local and Metropolitan Area Networks*, Prentice Hall (2000).

[**Stallings 2000b**] W. Stallings, *Operating Systems, Fourth Edition*, Prentice Hall (2000).

[**Stallings 2003**] W. Stallings, *Cryptography and Network Security: Principles and Practice, Third Edition*, Prentice Hall.

[Stankovic 1982]   J. S. Stankovic, "Software Communication Mechanisms: Procedure Calls Versus Messages", *Computer*, Volume 15, Number 4 (1982).

[Stankovic 1996]   J. A. Stankovic, "Strategic Directions in Real-Time and Embedded Systems", *ACM Computing Surveys*, Volume 28, Number 4 (1996), pages 751–763.

[Staunstrup 1982]   J. Staunstrup, "Message Passing Communication Versus Procedure Call Communication", *Software—Practice and Experience*, Volume 12, Number 3 (1982), pages 223–234.

[Steinmetz 1995]   R. Steinmetz, "Analyzing the Multimedia Operating System", *IEEE MultiMedia*, Volume 2, Number 1 (1995), pages 68–84.

[Stephenson 1983]   C. J. Stephenson, "Fast Fits: A New Method for Dynamic Storage Allocation", *Proceedings of the Ninth Symposium on Operating Systems Principles* (1983), pages 30–32.

[Stoica et al. 1996]   I. Stoica, H. Abdel-Wahab, K. Jeffay, S. Baruah, J. Gehrke, and G. Plaxton, "A Proportional Share Resource Allocation Algorithm for Real-Time, Time-Shared Systems", *IEEE Real-Time Systems Symposium*.

[Stokes 2007]   J. Stokes, *Inside the Machine*, No Starch Press (2007).

[Su 1982]   Z. Su, "A Distributed System for Internet Name Service", *Network Working Group, Request for Comments: 830* (1982).

[Sugerman et al. 2001]   J. Sugerman, G. Venkitachalam, and B. Lim, "Virtualizing I/O Devices on VMware Workstation's Hosted Virtual Machine Monitor", *2001 USENIX Annual Technical Conference*.

[Sun 1990]   *Network Programming Guide.* Sun Microsystems (1990).

[Svobodova 1984]   L. Svobodova, "File Servers for Network-Based Distributed Systems", *ACM Computing Surveys*, Volume 16, Number 4 (1984), pages 353–398.

[Talluri et al. 1995]   M. Talluri, M. D. Hill, and Y. A. Khalidi, "A New Page Table for 64-bit Address Spaces", *Proceedings of the ACM Symposium on Operating Systems Principles* (1995).

[Tamches and Miller 1999]   A. Tamches and B. P. Miller, "Fine-Grained Dynamic Instrumentation of Commodity Operating System Kernels", *USENIX Symposium on Operating Systems Design and Implementation* (1999).

[Tanenbaum 1990]   A. S. Tanenbaum, *Structured Computer Organization, Third Edition*, Prentice Hall.

[Tanenbaum 2001]   A. S. Tanenbaum, *Modern Operating Systems*, Prentice Hall (2001).

[Tanenbaum 2003]   A. S. Tanenbaum, *Computer Networks, Fourth Edition*, Prentice Hall (2003).

[Tanenbaum and Van Renesse 1985]   A. S. Tanenbaum and R. Van Renesse, "Distributed Operating Systems", *ACM Computing Surveys*, Volume 17, Number 4 (1985), pages 419–470.

[Tanenbaum and van Steen 2002]   A. Tanenbaum and M. van Steen, *Distributed Systems: Principles and Paradigms*, Prentice Hall (2002).

[Tanenbaum and Woodhull 1997]   A. S. Tanenbaum and A. S. Woodhull, *Operating System Design and Implementation, Second Edition*, Prentice Hall (1997).

[Tate 2000]   S. Tate, *Windows 2000 Essential Reference*, New Riders (2000).

[Tay and Ananda 1990]   B. H. Tay and A. L. Ananda, "A Survey of Remote Procedure Calls", *Operating Systems Review*, Volume 24, Number 3 (1990), pages 68–79.

[Teorey and Pinkerton 1972]   T. J. Teorey and T. B. Pinkerton, "A Comparative Analysis of Disk Scheduling Policies", *Communications of the ACM*, Volume 15, Number 3 (1972), pages 177–184.

[Tevanian et al. 1987a]   A. Tevanian, Jr., R. F. Rashid, D. B. Golub, D. L. Black, E. Cooper, and M. W. Young, "Mach Threads and the Unix Kernel: The Battle for Control", *Proceedings of the Summer USENIX Conference* (1987).

[Tevanian et al. 1987b]   A. Tevanian, Jr., R. F. Rashid, M. W. Young, D. B. Golub, M. R. Thompson, W. Bolosky, and R. Sanzi, "A UNIX Interface for Shared Memory and Memory Mapped Files Under Mach", Technical report, Carnegie-Mellon University (1987).

[Tevanian et al. 1989]   A. Tevanian, Jr., and B. Smith, "Mach: The Model for Future Unix", *Byte* (1989).

[Thekkath et al. 1997]   C. A. Thekkath, T. Mann, and E. K. Lee, "Frangipani: A Scalable Distributed File System", *Symposium on Operating Systems Principles* (1997), pages 224–237.

[Thompson 1984]   K. Thompson, "Reflections on Trusting Trust", *Communications of ACM*, Volume 27, Number 8.

[Thorn 1997]   T. Thorn, "Programming Languages for Mobile Code", *ACM Computing Surveys*, Volume 29, Number 3 (1997), pages 213–239.

[Toigo 2000]   J. Toigo, "Avoiding a Data Crunch", *Scientific American*, Volume 282, Number 5 (2000).

[Traiger et al. 1982]   I. L. Traiger, J. N. Gray, C. A. Galtieri, and B. G. Lindsay, "Transactions and Consistency in Distributed Database Management Systems", *ACM Transactions on Database Systems*, Volume 7, Number 3 (1982).

[Tudor 1995]   P. N. Tudor. "MPEG-2 Video Compression Tutorial". IEEE Coloquium on MPEG-2—What it Is and What it Isn't (1995).

[Vahalia 1996]   U. Vahalia, *Unix Internals: The New Frontiers*, Prentice Hall (1996).

[Vee and Hsu 2000]   V. Vee and W. Hsu, ""Locality-Preserving Load-Balancing Mechanisms for Synchronous Simulations on Shared-Memory Multiprocessors", *Proceedings of the Fourteenth Workshop on Parallel and Distributed Simulation* (2000), pages 131–138.

[Venners 1998]   B. Venners, *Inside the Java Virtual Machine*, McGraw-Hill (1998).

[Wah 1984]   B. W. Wah, "File Placement on Distributed Computer Systems", *Computer*, Volume 17, Number 1.

[Wahbe et al. 1993a]   R. Wahbe, S. Lucco, T. E. Anderson, and S. L. Graham, "Efficient Software-Based Fault Isolation", *ACM SIGOPS Operating Systems Review*, Volume 27, Number 5 (1993).

[Wahbe et al. 1993b]   R. Wahbe, S. Lucco, T. E. Anderson, and S. L. Graham, "Efficient Software-Based Fault Isolation", *ACM SIGOPS Operating Systems Review*, Volume 27, Number 5 (1993).

[Wallach et al. 1997]   D. S. Wallach, D. Balfanz, D. Dean, and E. W. Felten, "Extensible Security Architectures for Java", *Proceedings of the ACM Symposium on Operating Systems Principles* (1997).

[Wilkes et al. 1996]   J. Wilkes, R. Golding, C. Staelin, and T. Sullivan, "The HP AutoRAID Hierarchical Storage System", *ACM Transactions on Computer Systems*, Volume 14, Number 1 (1996).

[Williams 2001]   R. Williams, *Computer Systems Architecture—A Networking Approach*, Addison-Wesley (2001).

[Williams 2002]   N. Williams, "An Implementation of Scheduler Activations on the NetBSD Operating System", *2002 USENIX Annual Technical Conference, FREENIX Track* (2002).

[Wilson et al. 1995]   P. R. Wilson, M. S. Johnstone, M. Neely, and D. Boles, "Dynamic Storage Allocation: A Survey and Critical Review", *Proceedings of the International Workshop on Memory Management* (1995), pages 1–116.

[Wolf 2003]   W. Wolf, "A Decade of Hardware/Software Codesign", *Computer*, Volume 36, Number 4 (2003).

[Wood and Kochan 1985]   P. Wood and S. Kochan, *UNIX System Security*, Hayden (1985).

[Woodside 1986]   C. Woodside, "Controllability of Computer Performance Tradeoffs Obtained Using Controlled-Share Queue Schedulers", *IEEE Transactions on Software Engineering*, Volume SE-12, Number 10 (1986).

[Worthington et al. 1994]   B. L. Worthington, G. R. Ganger, and Y. N. Patt, "Scheduling Algorithms for Modern Disk Drives", *Proceedings of the ACM Sigmetrics Conference on Measurement and Modeling of Computer Systems* (1994).

[Worthington et al. 1995]   B. L. Worthington, G. R. Ganger, Y. N. Patt, and J. Wilkes, "On-Line Extraction of SCSI Disk Drive Parameters", *Proceedings of the ACM Sigmetrics Conference on Measurement and Modeling of Computer Systems* (1995), pages 146–156.

[Wulf 1969]   W. A. Wulf, "Performance Monitors for Multiprogramming Systems", *Proceedings of the ACM Symposium on Operating Systems Principles* (1969), pages 175–181.

[Wulf et al. 1981]   W. A. Wulf, R. Levin, and S. P. Harbison, *Hydra/C.mmp: An Experimental Computer System*, McGraw-Hill (1981).

[Yeong et al. 1995]   W. Yeong, T. Howes, and S. Kille, "Lightweight Directory Access Protocol", *Network Working Group, Request for Comments: 1777* (1995).

[Young et al. 1987]   M. Young, A. Tevanian, R. Rashid, D. Golub, and J. Eppinger, "The Duality of Memory and Communication in the Implementation of a Multiprocessor Operating System", *Proceedings of the ACM Symposium on Operating Systems Principles* (1987), pages 63–76.

[Yu et al. 2000]   X. Yu, B. Gum, Y. Chen, R. Y. Wang, K. Li, A. Krishnamurthy, and T. E. Anderson, "Trading Capacity for Performance in a Disk Array", *Proceedings of the 2000 Symposium on Operating Systems Design and Implementation* (2000), pages 243–258.

[Zabatta and Young 1998]   F. Zabatta and K. Young, "A Thread Performance Comparison: Windows NT and Solaris on a Symmetric Multiprocessor", *Proceedings of the 2nd USENIX Windows NT Symposium* (1998).

[Zapata and Asokan 2002]   M. Zapata and N. Asokan, "Securing Ad Hoc Routing Protocols", *Proc. 2002 ACM Workshop on Wireless Security* (2002).

Credits

Figure 1.11: From Hennesy and Patterson, *Computer Architecture: A Quantitative Approach, Third Edition,* © 2002, Morgan Kaufmann Publishers, Figure 5.3, p. 394. Reprinted with permission of the publisher.

Figure 5.13 adapted with permission from Sun Microsystems, Inc.

Figure 9.18: From *IBM Systems Journal,* Vol. 10, No. 3, © 1971, International Business Machines Corporation. Reprinted by permission of IBM Corporation.

Figure 11.9: From Leffler/McKusick/Karels/Quarterman, *The Design and Implementation of the 4.3BSD UNIX Operating System,* © 1989 by Addison-Wesley Publishing Co., Inc., Reading, Massachusetts. Figure 7.6, p. 196. Reprinted with permission of the publisher.

Figure 13.4: From *Pentium Processor User's Manual: Architecture and Programming Manual,* Volume 3, Copyright 1993. Reprinted by permission of Intel Corporation.

Figures 16.6, 16.7, and 16.9: From Halsall, *Data Communications, Computer Networks, and Open Systems, Third Edition,* © 1992, Addison-Wesley Publishing Co., Inc., Reading, Massachusetts. Figure 1.9, p. 14, Figure 1.10, p. 15, and Figure 1.11, p. 18. Reprinted with permission of the publisher.

Figure 19.5: From Khanna/Sebree/Zolnowsky, "Realtime Scheduling in SunOS 5.0," Proceedings of Winter USENIX, January 1992, San Francisco, California. Derived with permission of the authors.

Figure 23.6: is due to Dan Murphy (http://tenex.opost.com/kapix.html).

Sections of Chapter 6 and Chapter 18: From Silberschatz/Korth, *Database System Concepts, Third Edition,* Copyright 1997, McGraw-Hill, Inc., New York, New York. Section 13.5, p. 451-454, 14.1.1, p. 471-742, 14.1.3, p. 476-479, 14.2, p. 482-485, 15.2.1, p. 512-513, 15.4, p. 517-518, 15.4.3, p. 523-524, 18.7, p. 613-617, 18.8, p. 617-622. Reprinted with permission of the publisher.

Index